Tips

IDEAS FOR DIRECTORS

THE ART OF THEATER SERIES

Tips

Ideas for Directors

by Jon Jory

ART OF THEATER SERIES

SK

A Smith and Kraus Book

A Smith and Kraus Book
Published by Smith and Kraus, Inc.
177 Lyme Road, Hanover, New Hampshire, 03755
www.SmithandKraus.com

First Edition: May 2002
9 8 7 6 5 4 3 2 1

The Library of Congress Cataloging-In-Publication Data
Jory, Jon.
Tips: ideas for directors / by Jon Jory.
p. cm.
ISBN 1-57525-241-4
1. Theater—Production and direction. I. Title: Ideas for directors. II. Title.
PN2053 J625 2002
792'.0233—dc21
2002276538

ISBN-13: 978-1-57525-241-4

Contents

Casting

Vocabulary

The Play

The Team

Beginning

Table Work

Blocking

Working with the Actor

Rehearsal Process

Comedy

The Final Stage

The Director's Homework

To Sandy Speer,
Michael Dixon,
Paul Owen,
and all the comrades
of the long march.

Preface

In the days before methodology and training institutions, directors and actors shared what they knew through tips. "You saw it tonight, got any tips for me?" "Listen, I loved it but I have one tip." The young asked the old for them and the veterans gave them whether they were asked or not.

Growing up in a theater family in the 1940s and 1950s, I listened in on a lot of tips. I always thought it was a great way to pass on craft without the pretension. The person giving the tip was simply drawing it out of the well everybody drank from. Nobody assumed they had invented the tip; it was either general knowledge the other person had momentarily forgotten or something you would have learned anyway after you did a couple of dozen more plays. The combined wisdom of the tips didn't add up to a method and there was quite a bit of play in there, meaning that whatever it was worked most of the time, but there was always an exception. Luckily there would be a tip for the exception too; you just had to find the right person. By the time I had become a professional director in 1963, the tradition of the tip was in decline and I discovered that working directors very seldom talked together about the trade.

The net result of this was that though I worked constantly I improved slowly. I kept making mistakes (for years) that a tip or two by a peer or a veteran could have shortcutted.

For instance, I worked for thirty years before I really incorporated Stanislavski's "super objective" in my daily work. I'd read about it in my early twenties but I never understood its practical (and miraculous) application. It's annoying to realize you could have been doing better work for thirty years if someone had just given you a tip!

So here's a collection of them. Some I have heard in the family kitchen, a few at theater conferences, but most of them I fished out of the common well by making mistake after mistake in production after production. These are not the insights of genius; they are what I found out by spilling enough blood. If you've been working for a while they may serve as a reminder. If you're just setting sail, I'm confident they will save you a few theatrical scars.

So here they are out of the bars and hallways and dressings rooms and the crucible of rehearsal and performance. You probably have some to share. I wish to hell I'd run into you earlier.

Jon Jory

User's Guide

Please don't read this book straight through. My feeling is it would be like drinking too much espresso. These tips have been refined and compacted to be later expanded by your understanding and experience. Make the book your companion when you're working on a scene or a play. Skim for something that catches your attention to help you rehash today's rehearsal or plan for tomorrow's. When you have a problem section, moment, or actor, run through the appropriate reading until something strikes you. Is tomorrow your first meeting with a fight choreographer? There's a tip.

Now, there is a section on the director's homework. Everyone hates homework, so despite the fact it should start the book, I've put it last. When you're feeling strong or you're excited about an upcoming project, sit down in your favorite chair with your favorite snack and attempt it.

This book is meant to be a mentor and a reminder, not a chore. Dip into it and use what's helpful at the moment. Are these tips the only way to do a particular thing? Absolutely not. Have they been fire-tested? Yes, I use them every day that I work.

Remember, this isn't a method, it's a set of tools, and it's your task to find the right job for them.

Meanwhile, may I give you a tip?

What Is Directing?

The director delivers the story of the play clearly, evocatively, and emotionally to the audience using theatrical means. The director assists the actor in framing character and relationship so that the narrative's points are made. The director reveals meanings in the text based on the author's intent and his or her own response to the play. The director melds the visual world of the play and the intended meaning to give the audience a complete experience. The director assures a creative atmosphere for the work and manages time to create the best result. The directors, designers, and actors are a creative team with clear collaborative goals. Everything else is rehearsal.

Now that doesn't sound hard, does it?

Casting

THE CASTING JOB

Be good at it or perish. Cast the best actors not the best looks. Watch for an interior process and life. See if they make the transition. Can they handle language? Do they have an instinctive sense of what the play is about? Are they comfortable on stage or scared? How good is their technique? Is any of their work spontaneous or is it all "taped"? Do they show sufficient variety? Do they, as they say, have the chops? Do they make human contact, or are they too far back in their heads? Are they prepared or possibly (shhhh) lazy? Are they emotionally available? Can they move or are they lumps? Does their body respond to what their brain thinks? Are you just casting this person because you're attracted to him or her? If you're casting a major role, has the actor played major roles?

If I had to break it way down, I'd say cast for interior process and exterior technique. Technique without mind is abysmal. Mind without technique is useless.

Oh, and do they have a sense of humor? It's as necessary to tragedy as comedy.

Be on time, drink lots of water, be kind, be empathetic, and don't eat while they audition.

IN YOUR CASTING BRIEFCASE

1. A watch. You want to stay on time.

2. A file folder so you don't lose the casting schedule, your notes, or the actor's photo and résumé.

3. Two copies of the script. Someone will walk off with one of them.

4. Your own set of the sides (pages) from which you are auditioning.

5. Your cell phone.

6. Sharpened pencils and good pens.

7. Your address book and phone file.

8. Something to nibble on that isn't too messy and bottled water to drink, because dehydrated directors are snappish and lose concentration.

9. The necessary information on when the play goes into rehearsal, opens, and closes.

10. A notebook to write your impressions of each audition. If the call is a professional one done by a casting person, you'll receive a sheet giving the scheduled times, names of auditioners, and contact information.

AUDITION ETHICS

1. You, the director, should be on time.

2. You should be decently dressed in clean clothes as a mark of respect to the actors.

3. You should be polite, empathetic, and in no way misuse the power of your position.

4. You shouldn't spend a lot of time during the audition looking at the actor's résumé. It's rude.

5. You should rise when the person enters and again when they leave unless you are aged, infirm, or car sick.

6. Thank the actor courteously but do not give false hope.

7. If you have a ten- or fifteen-minute schedule per actor stay on it. If you're behind, catch up. Don't keep people waiting for long periods.

8. Always introduce the actor to the reader, if there is one.

9. Keep the audition table neat and clear of doughnut wrappers, half-eaten apples, and used tissues. You are inviting these actors to your temporary home.

10. Courtesy and warmth cost you nothing.

WORKING WITH
A CASTING PERSON

If someone is bringing the actors in for you, you want to be simpatico with that person. Explain your taste in actors as best you can. Explain what you see in the characters and the skills you see as necessary in playing them. If the production is high concept in some way, be clear about what you're doing. If you can give them an ideal example for the role (I would want Pacino) do so. (You won't get him but they might understand.) Take a minute to say what you don't want. "It's a musical, yes, but I don't want broad low-comedy musical acting."

When you start with a new casting person, explain in detail what you think about the first six or seven people who audition. That provides a benchmark so that the casting professional can understand your taste in actors. If you like an actor but don't know him, ask the casting person what she knows. After the call, it's polite (and often helpful) to ask what she thinks. Obviously, you must sometimes disagree. Listen to advice but know your own mind. Be honest, be clear, be nice, be demanding.

AUDITION MATERIAL

Pick the wrong scenes to audition the actors, you'll get the wrong actors. You need to see them handle what's key in the role and if they are capable of the hard stuff, the mad scene, the emotional outburst, the big monologue. If it's comedic, you want the funniest scene. If it's Shaw, the most complex speech. If it's commedia, you've got to see them move. If the character arcs from A to Z, you need to see both ends. If there's a killer-diller bear of a scene — the actor goes crazy, murders his child, and laughs hysterically — you might save it for the callback. Have two scenes with a third if they interest you. Keep each scene to a page and a half or less. If the role is minuscule, you might read the actor from a large role. Try to make sure the actors get the material at least three days beforehand. Don't let someone else (casting director, stage manager, personal assistant) choose the material. It needs to be the perfect vehicle to see what you have to see. In the callback, you may want to be reminded of their work on the material they did last time plus see new material. Take your time, choose carefully.

AUDITION NOTATION

Watch the audition. Don't spend the whole time writing. Devise a simple quick notation that the actor won't understand is she catches a glimpse.

O	Forgettable
Ø	No thought process
<	Handles text well
>	Handles text badly
♥	Loved her
~~♥~~	Hated her
B	Best so far
⇑	Moves well
⇓	Moves badly
i	Intelligent
D	Takes direction
~~D~~	Doesn't take direction
T	Good type
~~T~~	Wrong type
®	See for other roles
V	Good voice
Λ	Bad voice
©	Seems crazy

You don't have to write a short story. You just need essential information.

MAY I USE YOU?

When the auditioning actor winsomely asks you if he may use you during the audition (meaning may he make eye contact with you and imagine you are the other actor in the scene), your answer should be a charming version of no. Whenever I've let myself be talked into this mug's game, I always end up trying to act with the auditioner instead of analyzing the audition. If I don't respond to the actor, I have the vague discontent of not doing a good job. If I do, I become for that time another actor, which crowds out my director self. It's not your job. It's distracting, and I always end up self-conscious and irritable. This is one of those moments when you're going to end up feeling a little like the bad guy. Just say no.

DEFENDING THE READER

In most auditions for a specific play there is a reader, either paid or volunteer, who reads opposite the actor auditioning in the scene. Usually the reader sits downstage facing up to give as much focus as possible to the auditioner. The director has responsibilities to the reader. The first is to introduce the reader to the incoming actor (and that means full name). Next, the director watches out for the reader because actors without taste or discernment often abuse them. I've seen readers knocked out of their chairs, passionately kissed, their clothing torn.

At the first hint of the actor overstepping the bounds of the reader's comfort, the director must intervene; a clear "please don't do that" usually suffices. When the auditions conclude, it's nice when the director thanks and (when truthful) compliments the reader's work. I often ask readers about their opinions of the actors we've seen. Very often, they know something you don't.

WHAT THE RÉSUMÉ MEANS

You audition him. He's smooth, skilled, and utterly charmless. You wouldn't hire him. Forget the résumé. In the main, good actors audition well. Those who don't, you'd need to have seen them work. I never hire someone who auditions for a role badly on the basis that someone else says they're a good actor. That just doesn't work as percentage ball. Look at a résumé when you like the audition. It can then help in the following ways:

1. If you're casting a major role, it helps if the actor has played (and carried) major roles.
2. If it's comedy, you want comic credits. (Lots of good actors have zero comic sense.)
3. It's a big bonus if he or she has played in good theaters with good actors.
4. If you're iffy, the only help is to call someone whose taste you know and respect. Is that person on the actor's résumé?
5. Has he or she done the type of play you're casting?
6. Oh look, you've seen the actor's work and forgotten!

A résumé can help in a final choice between two actors. Mainly trust your eyes and ears, not the paper.

THINGS ACTORS WILL ASK YOU IN CASTING CALLS

1. "Is there anything you'd like to tell me before I start?" If there is, keep it brief.

2. "Is it all right if I start over?" Sure, if there's time.

3. "Which of these scenes should I do first?" If you care, say so.

4. "Did I make the adjustment you asked for?" I either tell the truth or am vaguely reassuring if I want to move on.

5. "How was that?" I always say, I got what I needed, which is true, negatively or positively.

6. They will tell you they have a cold, they just got the script last night, they knew your sister in kindergarten, they love the script, they admire your work, and they've always wanted to do this play. I smile and nod.

THE CALLBACK

You're down to three people to play Oedipus. (Actually, you can't find three people to play Oedipus, but we'll let it pass.) How do you handle bringing them back?

Well, for one thing you schedule one half hour for each returnee so you have time to work with him or her. And working with the callbacks is the point. Some directors just listen to the callbacks and make a decision. I can't understand that. Making the play isn't about how good the actor is, it's about your chemistry with the actor. It's about how you understand and react to each other in the creative process.

Give several adjustments to see how the callbacks take direction. Direct them physically. Give each one a move or two to see how their bodies work. Try some of the most emotionally demanding scenes. If it's beyond them, don't assume rehearsal will make the difference. See if they have a sense of humor. See what happens when you tell them to raise the stakes. If they seem defensive, they'll probably be defensive in rehearsal. If the role has extremes, see if they're willing to go there. This is no time to be shy.

THE MOMENT WHEN YOU CAST THE ACTOR

1. Forget, for a moment, special physical needs. Who's the best actor?

2. Is she emotionally connected? Can she do it or does she have to fake it?

3. Does he have presence? Any charisma?

4. What parts of the role will be hardest for her? Are these key moments and qualities?

5. Does he show ideas and feelings with his body? Is he physically connected?

6. Do you want to be in a room with this person for several weeks?

7. Does she have an intuitive sense of the role? You can't teach or direct that.

8. If it's a comedy, does he have the technique? It's hell teaching comedy technique in three weeks.

9. Is she charming? Most big roles need it.

10. Is he intelligent enough for you to enjoy working with him?

11. Can she handle the big moments?

12. Does he have enough energy?

13. Can she fill your theater with her acting?

CHOOSING THE ONE

The last auditioner exits. Done. Now, take a few minutes to look back through the photos and your notes, before others bombard you with opinions. Put the pictures in A piles (the person or persons you would cast), B piles (backups you would take), C piles (over your dead body). If you have an overwhelming sense that you should — no ifs, ands, or buts — cast a certain actor, don't second guess yourself, do it. Just to be sure you can face the music, hold up this paragon's picture and ask "any negatives?" Unless the others in the casting room make a point that changes your mind, make the offer. Sometimes extended chat can talk you out of the best actor.

If you have two or three choices, listen to all informed opinion, give yourself twenty-four hours for your subconscious to kick in, and then choose. Still confused? If you can, do another callback and/or call the references, particularly people you know personally. Still confused? Make a choice and never look back. Oh, remember as you choose, the virtues of a good mind, a body that reflects it, a cooperative nature, and the incalculable presence of skills and experience. At a certain point, go with your gut. Endless rumination won't help.

THE CASTING FILE

Start now. Start yesterday. An actor becomes ill —
you need an immediate replacement. The casting file.
A movie company comes to town, they need a six-
foot, three-inch actress who hails from Fiji. You can
help them. The casting file. When you see plays, take
a pen to write in your program. At home transfer
the actors you like to 3X5 cards and paste on their
program photo. At auditions take notes. If you can't
take the 8X10s (the theater wants them), ask if you
can come in and photocopy the audition day's photos. Then transfer your notes to the photo/résumé
and file them. Even if you're still at a university, keep
a file. You can make notes on people's acting class
work. The director with a strong casting file is miles
ahead. Categories are usually leading man, leading
woman, character man, character woman, juvenile,
ingénue. Also keep a musical file if that's your bag.
Every few years during a week when you're (shhhh)
out of work, weed it, and update it. You'll amaze
your employers and do better work.

Vocabulary

CIRCUMSTANCES

If real estate is about "location, location, location" then directing is "circumstances, circumstances." There are two kinds of circumstances to work with. The objective and (surprise!) the subjective. Objective circumstances are the text's facts based in situation (Jimmy and Bobbie are married), character (Jimmy has a temper, we see it in three scenes) and exterior facts (it's raining). Subjective circumstances will usually be characters' conversation about emotions, as in "I love you." As life has shown all of us, that's not half as clear as "it's raining." Subjective circumstances have subtext we need to penetrate.

An enormous part of director's job is to remind the actors of the circumstances, and that means not only the circumstances that surround the scene but those that impact the moment. Out of the circumstances the director finds not only the behavior but the blocking. List them, keep them near at hand, review them. They are the most powerful arrow in the director's quiver. Almost any acting problem can be assisted by them. The director doesn't need to know the answer, the circumstances usually provoke it.

BEATS

The beat is to acting and directing what the paragraph is to writing. The beat changes when the subject changes. There are textual and subtextual beats. The textual beat has no hidden meaning. We're talking about the weather with no hidden agenda. The subtextual beat might cover more than one subject. We talk about the weather and then we're to go for dinner but underneath, we're discussing our marriage. Put a bracket around the beat.

[ ]

This now becomes an identifiable unit to be worked on. Usually there will be actions, tactics, and obstacles for each character in each beat. Doing this work really helps the director understand the play, but it's arduous and very time-consuming. Usually the director does this work for key scenes and difficult moments. When you know a moment or exchange isn't working, go home and do the beats and analyze them. It will give you ways to attack the problem tomorrow.

THE ACTION

I'm going to call it what the character wants someone else to do, to feel, or to understand. (Some people would say I was describing an objective but let's
not quibble.) Now, couldn't we say the action is simply what the character wants? Yes, we want things
independent of other people, but in plays those
wants quickly run into others. By connecting the
action to another character you create the beginning
of the stimulus/response cycle that makes the best
acting and the best watching. It puts the scene
between the actors. The action clearly relates to the
meaning of the scene and the theme of the play. Each
beat has an action for each character in it. If the
action is "I want him to kiss me," you'll clearly
know when the action completes or fails. However
if the action oversimplifies what is going on, it may
demean the text. Particularly helpful to the director
is the query "To what end?" It opens up the complexities behind the simple action. You can examine a single moment for an action to solve a problem
in rehearsal. The alternative to an action is usually
acting for tone, which is far less specific and interesting.

THE OBSTACLE

My favorite. I find oh so many times that while the actor has some sense of what he wants, he is not nearly as clear about what is preventing him getting it. If you desperately need something but don't know or misjudge the obstacle, you will probably use the wrong tactics to get it. When energy and/or concentration flag, work with the actor on the obstacle. Ask the actor, "Jack, I know you want her to release you from the relationship but what do you feel is the obstacle to that?" Once that question is answered, you can move on to the tactic. "Well, if she still loves you, what tactics might encourage her to let you go?" Soon, through the leverage of the obstacle, you'll have the scene hopping. Use of the obstacle can lead you to solutions in the playing that you might never have conceived otherwise. Use it to do homework on a recalcitrant beat, page, or scene. You'll come back the next day with a fresh approach.

TACTICS

The tactic is the means used to complete the action. I want you to agree to give me the car father left you. Tactic One: I try to convince you he gave it to you out of spite. No dice. Tactic Two: I try to charm you into being generous. No dice. Tactic Three: I know you don't like conflict so I allow myself to get angry. No dice. Tactic Four: I get physical. You hand over the keys. The actor may change tactics but pursue the same action. If the obstacle is a strong one, it allows the actor to try different tactics, which creates the variety that holds our interest. When the work seems boring, it may be that you need to suggest another tactic. You don't even have to use the word *tactic*. Just put the actor on a new track to get what he wants. This directorial use of tactics has its limitations. Use this tool sparingly, and only on truly troubled moments. Overuse makes the characters manipulative and often that's wrong for the role.

TRANSITIONS

We're talking about how the actor gets from one idea to the next. Just to remind you, let's suppose the actor says:

> JIM: Listen, Andrew, we settled that.* Where's my coat?* What I really want to talk about is your marriage.* Good God, you won't believe what I just saw out the window.

Now, where you see the *, that's a transition from A to B. You can spend many happy hours in rehearsal watching the actors run them like so many stoplights. The net result of the actor dissing the transitions is to destroy sense, ignore rhythm, cripple our belief, and lose the opportunity for wonderful moments. The more important and central and emotional the speech the more harm can be done by the amazing disappearing transition. Now don't tell on me, but I often mark them in the text with a colored pencil. Do I insist on every transition? Of course not. But keep your eye peeled. You don't want a production devoid of thought process.

THE SUPER OBJECTIVE

Stanislavski first defined this rare tool for the director working with the actor. I spent twenty years of my career without understanding its value and when I finally did, it transformed my work. Here's the basic deal: The super objective is what the character wants above all. Since childhood, you have longed to build great buildings, to be an architect. Your working-class family think it's an impossible dream. You want a degree from Yale. You add a second job to save money. Now, each day brings its own challenges that are often remote from this larger goal, but whether you are being berated by the boss on the second job or listening to your boyfriend make plans for the two of you, the tonality of the scene is affected by the super objective as well as the immediate action. It's a wonderful clarifying tool to use with the actor. You love your boyfriend, but even on the romantic picnic he arranges, some part of you keeps him at a distance because of the super objective. Use it in your scene work, it will add dimension.

THE ARC

How the character changes from the beginning to the end. Obviously there will be different sorts of change. It might be a change in situation, a change in outlook, a change in relationship to others, to self, or to society. Does the character have to change? Oh, I hope so. Just how long can we watch Richard III murdering people with impunity before we long for a change or a restaurant? The practical point is that you don't want to be playing the end before it arrives, and you certainly don't want to be playing the beginning at the end. Yes, Samuel Beckett got away with it in *Godot*, but chalk that up to the exception that proves the rule. When you feel the beginning and end are clearly differentiated, try to find the fulcrum moment where the real change begins. That allows you to clarify other stations along the route. Soon you'll have a spine of change that can provide real assistance to the actor. There is also a necessity for change in key relationships that you may want to give thought to. The idea of change is in service to the continual need for variety on the stage, in the story, and with the characters.

THEME

For years I wanted to ignore it and get on to more practical matters. Finally, I began to realize that theme was the director's super objective. I saw that it unified my work and increased its power. It began to work for me as a kind of tie breaker. Should I do it this way or that way? Well, which way is more directly related to the theme? I've come to think of theme as the playwright's advice as to how to lead a better and more expansive life. Sometimes it means something we should do, sometimes something we shouldn't.

I realize I'll be pilloried for returning to the time when plays had to masquerade as moral lectures, but it helps me in expressing theme. I try to think of it as something about living a life that I would pass on to a beloved younger brother. When I can express it, I continually check my work on the play, on its characters and relationships, to sense the relationship of these things to the theme. It seems to keep me from pursuing paths and theatricalities that are beside the point.

CONFLICT

Use it as a tool all the time. Ask yourself, what's the conflict now? Ah yes, the staple of drama, comedy, and everything in between. Have you got it? Where do you need it? How would you define it? Its absence when its presence is necessary implies a misunderstanding of the circumstances. The root of the conflict may exist outside the scene or inside it, in the other character or in the self. Which is the case in the scene you're working on? In a practical sense, conflict often is synonymous with the obstacle to the action. Drama is like chess in that we know from the beginning the role conflict will play, but it's the tactics used in its service that fascinates us. Actors (who have so very much to think about and do) often lose track of it and need to be reminded. Often the nature of conflict at play in a scene is subtle but proves to be the key that opens the door. Yes, the balcony scene is a love scene, but its richest moments are steeped in conflict.

The Play

WHAT'S THIS?

I'm astounded at how often I have made rookie mistakes by forgetting what sort of play I'm doing. If it's a character comedy, build character that amuses and don't paste on door-slamming Marx Brother routines. Tragedy usually has a solemnity and austerity that would sink a behavioral drama like a torpedoed ship. Are you doing a spectacle, a folk tale, poetic drama, a mystery, a romantic comedy, or a metaphoric whatsit? Is the play primarily based in action, language, storytelling, physical comedy, or what?

It's hell when you don't use the right tools on the right play. This is why we need to see as much theater and film as we can. We need to understand the traditions of each form. If you haven't seen comedy of manners, you'll have to intuit its rhythms and its props. Seek out those who do know. Older actors are treasure troves of information. Block a language play like a farce, and no one will hear it. Treat romantic comedy like low comedy, and you'll push for laughs that aren't there. The rule is, know the form before you explode it.

TELLING THE STORY

I was directing years ago in a rep situation where I shared actors with an older British director who was later arrested for manslaughter and shall remain nameless. The day before we went into rehearsal, he tapped me on the shoulder with a pencil and asked if I was ready? Facing my first Shaw, I said I really didn't know. "Oh," he said, "there's an infallible way to know. The night before I go into rehearsal I find someone not connected with the theater, a bartender (apt in this case), someone in my hotel, and I say, 'Let me tell you a story.' I do the story of the play for them from memory, straight through, touching on all the characters and just before the end I look at my watch and say, 'Oh, my God, I've got to make a phone call.' If they say, 'Listen here, don't leave without telling me the end,' or anything of that kind, well, I'm damn well ready!" Not a bad idea, eh?

WHOSE PLAY IS IT?

Let's get real, sometimes it isn't anybody's play, it's everybody's . . . as in Chekhov. Most of the time, though, the question does apply. If it dramaturgically *is* someone's play (as in *Othello*) and you misjudge it, there's usually hell to pay. Big Daddy may be the most interesting role, but it's Maggie's play. When you give ultimate focus to a character or relationship that doesn't reveal the play's theme and emotional center, the production dithers, misses some wonderful opportunities, and, worst of all, doesn't pay itself off.

So, how do we know? Compare the function and destiny of the character to the play's theme. What happens in the last ten minutes usually makes the central character obvious. *School for Husbands* isn't about the young lovers getting together, it's about the father's seriocomic need to control. Once you feel you know, what then? You need to build the play toward that character's big moments and climax. You need to identify how other characters function to deliver the main character's story. You need to put extra effort into your work with the actor who centers the play.

WHAT KIND OF SCRIPT IS IT?

Different tools for different jobs. If you direct a situation comedy or farce as you would do a character comedy, woe betide you. If you believe it's not drama but melodrama, the critics will sharpen their claws. Do you sense the directorial difference between high comedy and satire? Go to the video store and educate yourself. You need to decide what this sort of play will mean to the work you do in rehearsal. If it implies a style, what is that and how will you communicate that to the actors? It also becomes a matter of emphasis. If you try to push an intimate biography of Eleanor Roosevelt until it becomes a spectacle, will the script bear it? Fantasy allows illogic, drama doesn't. Many's the time I've seen the director directing the wrong play when a little reflection might have saved him. You may disdain categorical thinking, but you do so in the theater at your peril. Brilliant minds successfully mix genres, but you need to know a genre to play with it. And, watch the "isms." If it's not realism but some other ism, what specifically is the acting difference? What is this play you're about to begin? First say why and then undertake how.

THE CENTRAL RELATIONSHIP

Some plays are about central characters (*Arturo Ui, A Man for All Seasons*), some are about central relationships (*A Doll's House, Jack and Jill*). In the former, you are usually dealing with a rise or fall, or a rise and fall. In the latter, you are dealing with a coming together or a falling apart. The first is about a central character's reaction to events. The second about the character's reaction to each other. In plays defined by a central relationship (*Antony and Cleopatra*) you need highly reactive actors who take and give intuitively and as a matter of technique. When the play is built around central relationships, it allows you to see the other characters by their function. How does what they do move the story of the key relationship forward? What must the others do to tell that story? It allows you, as the director, to focus in the right area. *Anthony and Cleopatra* isn't a play about Roman and Egyptian history. It's only incidentally a spectacle; it's about a relationship.

TRUSTING THE PLAY

Over and over again I heard my father and mother, veteran actors, back off overeager and overinventive young directors (myself included) by saying they weren't "trusting" the moment or the scene. Keep in mind that no matter how fascinating and fabulous we are, sometimes the text doesn't need embellishment. Clear examples are often found in staging songs in musicals. When the lyric and music is good, just get out of the way! The singer doesn't need to groom a wolfhound or tango; the song itself is the event.

Often the great scene and the great play only needs shrewd, almost invisible help from us. Take a hard look and decide whether you need to be the event ("Amazingly directed, wildly inventive!") or whether this play can basically do its own work. Make sure the play needs the extraordinary concept you have imagined. You want to release the play not obscure it. Watch an actor you think is too busy. Are you making the same mistake?

THE DIRECTOR
AND THE PLAYWRIGHT

I once wrote that directors who bar playwrights from rehearsal go to a special hell. I do know that in stressful circumstances it would not be untoward to ask for a day or two apart to prepare something for the playwright to look at. I believe that on a new play we are basically there to make what the writer conceives. Will there be tension and disagreements? Yes. Is it best to work through them together? Yes. Does the writer turn out to be right a majority of the time? Yes. Should the writer ever speak directly to the actors in rehearsal? Yes, they will anyway over a beer. Should the writer ask you first? Yes. Many times I ask the writer to say something to them that she has said to me the night before because I loved the way she said it. Sometimes you must rephrase the playwright's comments so that the actors can absorb the idea on their own terms. It is always best that the writer and director have hammered out an approach before rehearsal, but it isn't always possible, and there are problems generated in the moment. You need to trust the complexity of the writer, director, actor equation. It pays off.

OVERLAPPING

Two or more actors speaking simultaneously. Like any strong spice, you have to add it to the dish carefully. Because the usual result is you don't hear either person, it is best used when the dialogue isn't crucial but the emotions are high. Playwrights love this device, which just goes to show they don't know everything. Careful rehearsal can get one actor to pull down for a key sentence from the other actor, but it's time intensive. The overlap is usually there to signal tempestuous temperaments who are so fired up they can't wait to have their say. Good idea. Usually the overlap is shallow, meaning Actor B starts in three words before Actor A is finished. Used with discretion it gives you a different sound to play with and contributes to a sense of spontaneity. Overused, it's simply irritating and annoys the audience. It could work (for a while) as a character trait. Keep it in your arsenal, but don't haul it out as a party trick.

INTERCUTTING THE LINES

Sometimes you can get extra energy by intercutting two speeches.

DAN: Listen! I don't care what you say. Pack up and get out.
DORA: I'm sorry. I'm not leaving. And you heard me!

INTERCUT:
DAN: Listen!
DORA: I'm sorry.
DAN: I don't care what you say.
DORA: I'm not leaving.
DAN: Pack up and get out.
DORA: And you heard me!

It can make a declarative section of text much more interactive and involve the actors more powerfully, driving the pace at a point where you feel you need it. Keep your eye open for these possibilities. Probably not an option with the playwright in the room.

THE CLASSICS

In one hundred and fifty words? Sure. You can avoid many misfortunes by breaking down the scenes, using actions and obstacles and subtext as you always have (and don't tell me there's no subtext in Shakespeare!). Manners (as in "which fork?") have a lot to do with these plays; either research them or invent them. Making clear what the play is about is a good thing. If you can't handle more than four people onstage at the same time, avoid them. Make sure everyone speaks clearly and not too quickly. I'm not kidding. Block the play early; it's going to be harder than you think. Make sure you know what they're saying. Combat takes a lot of rehearsal time, plan for it. Dance takes a lot of rehearsal time, plan for it. Don't make people do the play on a steep rake; it hurts their knees. Cast actors who move well. Cast strong voices. Cast for experience. Make the set less complex rather than more complex — you've got enough problems. Don't try to be too clever; these writers are smarter than you are. Go for clarity and the play will save you.

SHAKESPEARE

1. Playing the situation and circumstances honest and straight works here as in any play.

2. Other than generally having good manners, kings, queens, and dukes don't behave in any particular way.

3. Make points not tone.

4. Study scansion but don't deify it.

5. Shakespearean clowns are God's revenge on the audience.

6. No matter what anybody says, cut.

7. Don't do the play until you can say all the lines in contemporary English.

8. Don't forget to work on relationships.

9. Enjoy the language; it's the only time the actor will ever say *incarnadine*.

10. Clarity works.

11. Don't substitute concept for understanding or complexity.

12. Only agree to do the plays you like.

13. Fight to get a verse coach.

14. Don't do it with the wrong actors or inadequate rehearsal.

15. Simplicity, clarity, heart.

DIRECTING THE BIG MUSICAL

This process will come as something of a shock to the director used to shaping the whole production and as a wonderful challenge to your organizational skills. Unless the rehearsal period is unusually generous, you will be directing book scenes in one room, the choreographer will be working in another, and the music director may be inhabiting a third. What's being created where you're not? You'll only have a general idea based on preshow meetings. You may be so busy you won't know until everything begins to come together much later. Shock number two is that your work on the book scenes isn't what the audience comes to see. They are paying their money for the numbers. Shock number three, skilled musical actors work differently than the actors you're used to. Prepare yourself to be a member of a team. Organize the time available to the last minute. Try to be in the room with the choreographer as much as possible. The big scenes with twenty-five actors, singers, dancers, and three songs and a dance number will take much longer than you think. Get blocked early so you have time to give input in the other areas. Stay calm, control your ego, enjoy yourself.

WHY DO YOU CARE?

You've got the job. You know what the play is about. You go into rehearsal Wednesday. Do you actually give a damn? This is the directorial equivalent to Stanislavski's searing question, "Do you love art or only yourself in art?" The best work is done by directors passionate about the play's ideas, politics, relationships, humanity, or morals because, more often than not, lukewarm feelings make lukewarm work. Now, with the way the world functions, you won't always be able to select the play you direct. Sometimes you may have to do it for (shhhh) the money or the entré.

There are, however, no excuses. It's your job to care about the play you do. You need to find something in it that speaks to your own life and makes the work personal to you. Do not go into rehearsal without having found a way to care. It may be some aspect of the message. It could be a troubled relationship you know from experience is worth saving. It may be some failed and parallel aspect of your own life that can now become art rather than regret. Theater as another day at the office is profoundly dispiriting.

The Team

WARNING THE PRODUCER

Dear friends, gather with me around the fire. Now, don't surprise the people who have hired you to direct a play with a production plan they could never have anticipated. If you're going to do *A Doll's House* on ice, tell them up front. This includes counting on things they didn't know about that cost lots of money. I was once told midway in rehearsal that certain lighting instruments were crucial that cost $75,000 apiece. We didn't buy them, and we didn't rehire the director. If the play needs unlisted extras, special materials, nudity not found in the text, tell the producer very, very early. If you're adding profanity or planning not to do the play as a comedy or hoping to perform the second act in the parking garage, do it when you're hired. The producer not only needs to hear your plans but is flattered to be included in your creative process. Openness will prevent catastrophe. Tell now. Tell all.

WORKING WITH THE ARTISTIC DIRECTOR

You will be working in other directors' theaters. Some are jealous and fearful of other talents; some are generous and confident that your success will enhance theirs. The most important quality for a guest director is openness. Make clear to the artistic director your goals with the play. Ask for budget information so you can be sure your ideas are affordable. Ask for any tips she would like to give on working with the staff. Make it clear that the artistic director is welcome at any time in your rehearsals. If you have cast the play independent of the theater's leader, talk a little about the actors. If roles have been precast by the artistic director, ask for advice about the performers. If the artistic director has absented herself from your rehearsals, drop in to see her midway and talk honestly about the work and your progress. If she visits your rehearsal, ask for notes. The key is not to be defensive and protective. We can all use informed help. After the opening, return once more to thank her for the support. Later write a thank-you note. A little courtesy goes a long way.

PREREHEARSAL SET DESIGN

Talk about the text. Say what you feel the play's about, what it means to you, why you're attracted to it, why it's a good time to do this play. Ask for the designer's reaction to the play before the conversation moves toward specifics. You might mention whether you're interested in an abstracted or realistic take on the material. Is everyone agreed on the period you will use for the production? After this broad view, you can move on to the script's necessities of place and space. Hopefully at an early meeting, research (photographs, paintings, history) will become part of the proceedings. Later on there will be renderings or, more likely, a model of the set to examine and react to. Though we are discussing sets, as many of the design team as possible should be involved. Obviously costume meetings will be concurrent, but whenever possible gather as a team rather than separate meetings with you the director. When the model does arrive, you need to go through the script with the designer to make sure the ground plan functions well. Above all, remember the designer is a creative artist and collaborator. Don't tell, ask.

LEVELS AND RAKES

For plays with swirling movement, you can make do on a flat floor, but the visual opportunities of levels are eternally seductive. I love rakes because they give you infinite levels, but I would be remiss not to add how actors over thirty hate them. (I've lost two actors at awkward times because of rake injuries.) Rakes are wonderful for composition because actors are seen against the floor. Second and intermediate levels open up staging and give it dimension. The downside is the size of the build it takes to get them. Levels can also be achieved more austerely. I've worked with climbing poles, ladders, furniture bolted to the back wall, trapped floors, ropes, trapezes, and footholds in walls — you name it. Always review mentally what the levels you imagine will look like as structures. It won't happen often, but allow me to whisper the word *ungainly* as a warning. If you think of the production as a three-dimensional shape, it helps you see the possibilities.

PREREHEARSAL COSTUME DESIGN

In the theater the traditional attitude is that the set designer is the unspoken, unelected chairperson of the design team. Although the costume designer is present from the beginning, she usually keys off the set designer's lead as to period, style, and color. (Obviously not every team has the same pecking order.) Once a general approach has been decided on, you will have several meetings with costumes alone. Once again, discuss the play and the characters prior to any conversation about costume specifics. For heaven's sake don't start saying what people should wear. The designer will think of wonderful things you could never imagine. If you have ideas about color palette, it's often helpful to find a painting containing the tonalities and range you're interested in. (Please God, not another red, white, and black production!) Once renderings and swatches of fabric are part of the discussion, react but try to explain why. Return to discussion of character. Are the renderings general or specific in their handling of character? Remember that saying what you do like is as helpful as saying what you don't like. At the right moment, be decisive so the show can go into the shop on time. It's rehearsal now. You and the designer enter a new period.

PREREHEARSAL STAGE MANAGEMENT

The first-rate stage manager who is on your side will be your greatest asset. Make friends and stay friends. He'll get you out of many a tight spot. Once again, talk concept and the idea of the play with the stage manager; he likes and needs to be in on it. Share any and all design information. If the stage manager is available for design meetings, so much the better. The stage manager obviously needs the designer's drawings to tape the floor for rehearsal. Discuss general rehearsal strategy. How long will you work at the table? Will you block consecutively? When is the best time for production meetings? Will you schedule three days ahead or only one? How will costume fittings affect the schedule? Discuss any useful information you can convey about the actors. Special needs? Is anyone hard of hearing? Is someone unusually shy? It will help the stage manager help you. Chat a bit about rehearsal props and rehearsal clothes that will be needed early. Does the rehearsal furniture have particular qualities? If you have small obsessions (I adore having sharpened pencils available), now is the time to come clean. Build this relationship. The committed stage manager makes you look good.

PREREHEARSAL WITH ACTORS

Well, maybe. Sometimes. A lot of times, geography separates, or neither of you are available. Plus you don't want to get single actors too far ahead of the group lest they fall into the "teacher's pet" category, which can be divisive. If we're talking about one of the great roles, as in *Hamlet, Mother Courage, Lear, Hedda Gabbler,* it's a different ballgame. These roles are so complex and dominant that the director and actor need to get on the same page before rehearsal. You'll often need to build concept around the actor's skills, quality, and ideas.

I once made the mistake of withholding a strong concept from an important actor playing one of these monster roles until the first rehearsal and was told in no uncertain terms he wasn't going to do that. Not so easy to replace a Richard III. You might tell actors early about accents, playing guitars, special skills (juggling, fire eating), nudity, dangerous falls, difficult costumes, or steep rakes. This is, of course, all a judgment call, but think through the necessities of what you're doing. You might, however, contact the actor to tell her you're glad she's doing the role.

PREREHEARSAL WITH LIGHTS

Usually the key decision to be made between the director and lighting designer is whether the light is to be realistic in the sense that the play is lit by logical sources according to the time of day, or expressionistic, allowing the designer to support the emotional or symbolic tenor of the scene. Once that is discussed, there may be conversation about the desired quality of the light. Will it be cold, warm, saturated color, or perhaps a sort of light favored by a particular painter, photographer, or filmmaker? If it is a play of many scenes, this could occupy a meeting of some length. Beyond this, the director might have an effect or two in mind (as will the designer), and conversation will arise about single moments needing special handling. All this will be more than enough for a good beginning as I am making the assumption that you began by discussing the play. It is always a wonderful plus if the designer is around for early rehearsals, though in many professional venues the director may not see the lighting designer again until just before tech.

RELATING TO THE SOUND DESIGNER

Some directors used to working in smaller venues will have scraped together their own sound scores throughout their careers. Your first adventure with a professional sound designer can be a revelation. Once again, resist the temptation to simply tell him what to do. If you have a genre or a particular composer or songwriter or category of sound in mind, trot it out but be willing to have your mind and taste expanded. Give the designer some hints about the complexity of the work. Is this a few ambient cues and scene music, or is this a whole lot of under-scoring and composition? Explain the script, your take on it, and any sort of sound you already know you don't want. Once in residence, the utopian sit-uation is to have the designer in the rehearsal room with the equipment so the sound is integrated early into the actor's work. Avoid the horrible tech moment when the actor turns front and says coldly, "You're going to play those chickens under my death speech?" Keep up with what the designer is doing. Schedule adequate time for you to listen to the options (and you should be hearing options!), and discuss whether the search needs to go on. Give the sound designer sufficient time to work cues in tech. Don't start yelling the first time a cue is attempted.

RELATING TO THE CHOREOGRAPHER

Many basically straight plays still demand the talents of the choreographer. Let's say you're doing a Marivaux and the author tells you the play ends with a "general dance." Even though this only affects two minutes of stage time, hire the choreographer early enough so that she may attend design meetings. Space and clothes will need her input. If she cannot attend, send her early renderings. Have her come to auditions and let her dance the actors who are your finalists so as to give you input. You may not know what form the dance should take, but at an early meeting, talk about the play, ideas for style, ideas for design, the mood you hope the dance will establish, and anything about period she may need. If the play is cast without her, describe their movement abilities as best you can. Two crucial things: have her attend costume fittings (can't dance in that hobble skirt, honey?) and make sure you attend her rehearsals with the cast so you can give guidance about what you like and what you don't. Don't tell her "how" but react.

RELATING TO THE FIGHT DIRECTOR

A rule of thumb. A fight taking one minute of stage time between two participants (weapons, not fists) will take four hours of rehearsal *with* the fight director and daily repetition after he's gone. Add an additional hour for each added fighter. It's time- consuming. I usually bring in the fight director in the second week when we all know more about the shape of the play and characterization. Let the fight director suggest the weaponry used and explain why. Good people in this field will want to know as much about the design, your take on the play, and the evolving sense of character as possible. Pick a fight director with a great reputation for actor safety. Check references. Agree on a tone for the fight. Is it funny, awkward and brutal, elegant, dashing and romantic, or nasty and scary? As you watch the rehearsals, counsel the fight director as to how long the fight should be. Sometimes, out of a fascination with the form, the fight becomes overextended and doesn't hold. Better a brilliant fight at forty seconds than a workmanlike fight at two minutes. Schedule fight rehearsal early before people are tired. Bring the fight director back for the move onto the set and the tech.

WORKING WITH THE PROP MASTER

Props, more's the pity, often seem to be at the low end of the design hierarchy. Don't make them feel that way. If they haven't been in the room for set and costume design sessions, seek them out and have the same conversations about the play. Be ready at the first meeting to talk about any specialty props needed (the exploding casserole, the mysteriously disappearing ship model, the hamburger that lights up). Shortly thereafter you need to go through the show. You, well-prepared director that you are, have a prop list (with page numbers) that you've made. She, excellent and informed prop master, has hers. Compare. Ask questions. Exude charm. If your charm has landed, go over a wish list of props you'd like to have in rehearsal — understanding, of course, just how busy this person is. If you can possibly manage it, ask for a prop parade a couple of days before tech. Better to criticize a prop now than in front of everyone. Always ask the actor to try using a prop at least twice before accepting his idea it won't work.

WORKING WITH DRAMATURGS

Dramaturg? You need one. Directors have tradition-
ally been lone minds and sensibilities. How much
better to have someone on your side to check in with.
By sharing with the dramaturg your ideas about the
script (and asking for hers) and character and concept you hope to get back wonderful questions that
help you revise (and sometimes abandon) your
ideas. You'll get key pieces of research that deepen
your understanding.

Later in the process something even more helpful occurs; the dramaturg reminds you of your earlier ideas that you have forgotten about in the heat
of battle so you can be sure they make it to the stage.
Yes, it's often useful to have someone defend *your*
ideas against you. The dramaturg can also be a useful and informed audience by telling you what she
sees onstage during rehearsals and what she takes it
to mean. We all know the director loses objectivity,
and when that happens, a good dramaturg can rein-
state it.

TECHNICIAN MACHO

I'm using this term for both male and female technicians and, sometimes, designers. This term charac-
terizes an attitude they've developed after years of
being excluded from the artistic process. It goes like
this: "All that matters to me is to know clearly and
on time precisely what you want me to design, build,
cut, drape, hang, or prop. 'Why' is your problem.
You make the decisions you need to make, and I'll
get it done for you. Don't give me a long rigmarole,
just give me the facts."

Because these theater workers have little control
over concept or how their work is used or rejected,
they find it safer and less punishing to adopt an "at
arm's length" attitude that seems cynical. But even
moderate gestures of inclusion penetrate this armor
easily. The fact that you are willing to share ideas
and empathize with their difficulties, let alone
respect their contributions, will make them go the
extra mile for you. You may also find they have ter-
rific ideas for the faltering scene or can easily put
their finger on a problem. Include them.

WIGS

There are probably two dozen really good wig-makers working in the American theater. The odds are that none of them is working on your production. Bad wigs, my friend, are the wrath of God made manifest. They can turn lovely looking humans of both sexes into walking jokes. On top of that, good wigs are very expensive (like good shoes or boots for your production), and a show full of them will eat your costume budget like locusts.

Your local wig shop with its witty creations made from old sports-drink bottles will not be a good basis for your brilliantly researched thesis production of *She Stoops to Conquer*. What to do? Well, if you're in charge, be careful about selecting big-wig shows in small-budget situations. Can you move the period to a nonwig century or decade? Will it be too horrible to use their own hair? Can you narrow it down to two good wigs? Can you get an airplane ticket out of the country? Wigs cost a lot of money, shoes cost a lot of money. Perhaps you should have the wigs and let the actors go barefoot.

WORKING WITH
PUBLIC RELATIONS

All of us want people in the seats and care about the look and message of the promotional materials. The director can assist both areas. Shortly after beginning work with a new theater, drop in on the marketing department and say, "Anything you guys would like me to do to publicize the play, I'm up for?" Many directors remain remote and have to be hunted down for a radio interview that they then refuse because it would interfere with their lunch break. From personal experience I can tell you producers remember the director who assists. Do whatever is asked with alacrity and a smile. Work that makes money can open doors for the director. Talk to the PR staff about your ideas for the play. Their delight in your attention will often allow you more say in the graphics and hyperbole surrounding your production. You may get input into the press releases and program notes. It gives you the opportunity to create an artistic whole of your production and the work that creates the bridge between it and the audience. It's a wonderful opportunity.

Beginning

THE DIRECTOR'S OPENING REMARKS

It's the first day of rehearsal. The actors are gathered at the table with scripts, sharpened pencils, expectation, and dread. What should you say? Well, things you believe for a start, why this text at this theater at this time? Tell them why you like the play (it's your *job* to like the play). Tell them what you think it means. Telling the story of the play in a couple of minutes will often reveal your take on it. Do you have a production concept? Let them in on it.

Not only your remarks but your manner will be noticed. "What sort of person is this?" they're thinking. (A prepared one, I hope.) I'd suggest you work from notes and keep it between five and fifteen minutes. Let's not bore them to tears. You can ask if they have questions at this point, but they may not. Your talk usually takes place after the designers have done show and tell, but it's your call. The point is to stimulate, hopefully to excite, and to "set the bar" for the work ahead. Don't bore, pontificate, or over explain. Be your charming self and strike to the heart of the play.

INTRODUCING THE DESIGNERS TO THE ACTORS

Actors love designs and by inference the designers who create them. Whenever possible, the set, costume, prop, light, and sound designers should have a defined time to present their ideas, renderings, plans and models to the actors on the first day. It's exciting for everyone and helps set the compass for the cast. A preparatory meeting between designers and director lets everyone talk and rehearse before presenting to the actors. Usually one begins with the set designer who, at least in the professional world, is considered the organizing force and first among equals. Everyone should be brief! The whole presentation of ideas for the production may last an hour. The actors should be encouraged to ask any questions they may have, and usually each presentation is applauded. Often the costume designer lays renderings on the floor, and the actors walk around them. There is a sense of ceremony and tradition here that creates a valuable unity.

THE DRAMATURG'S TALK

We all know what a dramaturg does, eh? Well maybe I'll just remind myself. Finds plays. Helps playwright and director develop the play for production. Helps the actors and audience make sense of the experience. Provides research. Ordinarily, unless the author and play are simple as dirt, the dramaturg would speak for up to an hour on the first day.

The director and dramaturg are in tune, and each knows, more or less, what the other will say. The dramaturg will give background on the play, author, period, and issues. He will explore the play thematically and relate that to the author's other work. The dramaturg may suggest reading for the actors and will clarify how he will relate to rehearsals and the company. Pass outs may be provided. This should heighten the sense of a meaningful adventure and contribute to the creative drive and process of all assembled. By now, people should be trampling each other to get at that script!

HOUSEKEEPING

After the director, designers, and the dramaturg have
spoken, it is time to get a few details out of the way
before the first reading. The dispatching of these
details is usually handled by the stage manager. This
allows that important personage visibility with the
actors and substantiates her authority. A strong stage
manager (but not an officious one) is the director's
best friend. If it is a union production, there will be
union business. If not, there are phone numbers and
addresses to gather, rehearsal schedules, tech schedules, and performances to explain. There is probably a word about costume fittings. A list of contact
information for people working on the production
should be passed out. If people are new to the area
where rehearsals are held there may be lists of
restaurants and parking information to pass along.
Who do actors call if they're confused about the next
day's rehearsal? Revised scripts may need to be
passed out. The director should allow the stage manager center stage. Now, a ten-minute break and then
the first reading.

LISHING LEADERSHIP

At the beginning of rehearsal, it is comforting to the actors to know their director is warm, human, and in charge. They hope the director will know the play and its roles and will set parameters for the coming explorations.

1. Know all the participants' full names.

2. Be prepared to make introductions.

3. Excite the actors about their roles and the play.

4. At this point, it's your job to know the script better than they do.

5. The actors will notice if what you say is useful to them and the process. Don't blather.

6. If you don't speak well extempore, work from notes.

7. If you are asked something and don't know, say so. But know tomorrow.

8. Have and follow a schedule. They will be watching how you manage time.

9. Give people breaks on time and go back to work promptly when they are over.

10. Say hello and good-bye to each member of the cast.

Actors form impressions of the director early. Don't waste the opportunity to make that impression positive.

Table Work

WORK AT THE TABLE

Work at the table is for figuring things out before the noise, froth, movement, and psychological density of rehearsal make reflection more difficult. Such work might last anywhere from five hours to seven days (based on 90 to 150 rehearsal hours). The director's job is to make connections between the play's meanings and each character's nature, behavior, scenes, and moments. Guidance toward or away from original instincts might be given. The director's view is clarified and related to specific text. The actors' (and hopefully) designers' views are sought and discussed. Back story, as it is relevant, is touched on. Questions are asked. Fears are spoken. Terrible ideas are mercifully dispatched. Bonding takes place. Coffee is slurped. The director's obvious hard work, discernment, and common sense are admired. Time is taken to work painstakingly through the script and close with an uninterrupted read-through in whatever number of hours has been allotted. The longer and more complex the play, the longer the time at the table.

GOOD TABLE WORK

1. There is a palpable attempt to interest and excite the actors about the play and the parts.

2. The atmosphere is such that everyone feels free to ask questions and express opinions, but the process seems gently guided. No stepping on each other's process and a sense that ideas and feelings can be engaged.

3. Agreement is reached on helpful parameters for the work so the discussion can be focused.

4. The director earns a leadership role by being helpful, clear, prepared, and text-proficient.

5. There are some good snacks at the coffee break.

6. People feel a plan of action is being developed by the group in an atmosphere of concentration, brevity, clarity, charm, and respect. (Plus a few good metaphors never hurt.)

TABLE MISTAKES

What should we avoid while working at the table? Let's see.

1. Pretension. This is usually the actor's view of heady, abstract lectures he or she can't see as directly useful.

2. Disorganization. The sense that the table work is out of control. Too long spent here. No time spent there. Theater stories from the director's career. A feeling that what's discussed is random and offhand. Such work leads to a loss of respect, and at the beginning of the process: Dangerous.

3. Faking. You don't really know the script and you're pretending you do. Uh-oh.

4. Egomania. The sense that we have here the puppets and the puppet master. The actors begin evasive action.

5. Deadening specifics. "This will be like this." "You'll say this this way." Gives the horrible sense that there is to be no room for discovery, imagination, and poetry in the process.

6. Murderous earnestness. No fun, no jokes, no playing with ideas, no joy, no passion, no surprises. Help!

WHAT THE ACTOR WANTS FROM TABLE WORK

1. A fascination with the play and an excitement about the role.

2. A sense of the whole and its meanings. How does my role function within that?

3. Am I on the right track? If I'm not, give me guidance in starting a new thought process.

4. What sort of director is this? What's her take on the play? Is she an auteur or a collaborator? Is she any good? Does she have the chops?

5. What, for starters, do I need to know about the style, relationships, structure, back story, dialect, function, and problems to get started on my process?

6. Am I liked and respected? Will I be safe taking risks here?

7. Who are these other actors? Will there be a sense of ensemble? Do we have a common vocabulary?

8. What should I work on first?

TABLE PSYCHOLOGY

We're just talking common sense. You should sit somewhere in the middle so you don't inhibit discussion by playing lord or lady of the manor. Allow people to bring coffee to the table; you want concentration but in an informal atmosphere. Try to seat people who have big scenes together next to each other. Encourage people to switch chairs during the work to make contact. If you know there is a difficult actor, try to seat the charming diplomats around him. On the breaks, talk to a different actor each time, particularly those new to you: You're trying to build working relationships. Make sure you introduce the stage manager and anyone else joining you at the table. At a certain point in the table work, some actors will rise and work on their feet. It's usually a sign that it's nearly time to start the blocking. As mentioned before, it's best to finish this phase with an uninterrupted read-through after two detailed work-throughs.

ASKING QUESTIONS AT THE TABLE

Questions are the heart of table work. If you, the director, come to the process with ten questions for each actor tied to moments in the text, you are wonderfully prepared. Ask why something happens. Ask why it happens at *that* moment. Ask what a character wants in a key scene. Ask why the play has its title. Ask whose play is it. Ask what each character has to lose. Ask if the people are really in love. Ask what can be learned by the set description. Ask what the play's about. Ask what the scene's about. Ask what the character's plot function is. Ask why he does this instead of that. Ask what the back story is on a relationship or a key event. Ask what blindness or race-car driving or moving to South Dakota means as metaphor in the play. Ask what the most important events are. Ask how the characters change. Ask why it's funny. Ask what's political about the play. Ask, ask, ask, ask, and then ask.

TALKING THE RELATIONSHIPS

Plays are plots explicated through relationships (well, usually). Delving into the relationships is a key component of table work. It is difficult, for example, to block the first scene of *Three Sisters* without a discussion of each sister's relationship to the other two. There may not be talk time for *every* relationship, but certainly the major ones the plot turns on. What crucible has produced the relationship? How does the relationship change as the play develops? What are the key moments in it? How do others react to the relationship? How does this relationship impact on other relationships?

Blocking cannot be undertaken without this patterning. On stage, we move in relationship to things but, more important, to other people. This work is also an opportunity for the actors to begin a dialectic with each other with the director as moderator. All such discussions should refer to support for the ideas *in the text*. One person shouldn't dominate such work. Sharing is crucial. The actors will learn, the director will learn, and an energy and excitement will build that will soon lead you away from the table.

TALKING THE SUBTEXT

So, you're at the table and the murderer (as yet unrevealed) and her victim (who thinks she knows) are discussing how to make an omelet. While everybody is seated and in the mood for chat, you may want to discuss the subtext. In fact, you may even want to speak it instead of the lines for a key section. We're all on the same page as to what the subtext is, aren't we? What the characters are really thinking and/or communicating rather than what they're saying. Why do this at the table? Well, for one thing, the actor's ego is less in play at the table. They mind less saying, "I don't know." For another, the subtext often drives the blocking, and we need to have begun it first. Most important, it assists the buy-in, penetration, and interest, which make a good production. Remember, the subtext allows the actor a direct portal to the necessary interior process. Often if it isn't discussed at the table, it never will be. Look for emotionally dense or seemingly flat and obvious sections of text and do this work! Yes, you'll still be involved with subtext in the third week, but the table is its natural and primary home.

RELATING MOMENTS

Anytime you can point out to the actor how something said or done early in the script leads to a key or defining moment later in the text, do it. It is for this precise task of tying moments together that table work exists. You might want to write a dozen or so such connections down and have them in front of you at the table so you don't forget. Actors also love to hear about contrasts. "See how this moment provides a contrast to what we've known of the character so far?" Also you will want the actors to start thinking about the arc. How is she different at the end than in the beginning? You should also be working to define relationships in the play and how they change during the course of the action. You can point out traps as in, "We have to be careful that Iago's manner doesn't imply that Othello must be stupid or unaware." Compliment people when they do something that shows they are on the right track.

Blocking

BLOCKING THE PLAY

A crucial, even defining, skill and one of the most difficult to dissect. Blocking is often behavioral, as in going to the kitchen for a cup of coffee. It is psychological in the human and emotional needs that drive it. It is aesthetic, giving pleasure through composition of bodies in space. It is architectural in the relationship of the actors to the set and the building. It provides focus by directing our eye and ear to the necessary place. It provides physical punctuation for the text. It reveals character through its details and story through its juxtapositions. It makes metaphor that enhances meaning. It creates rhythm that deepens attention and gives pleasure. It clarifies what happens between people and is a sort of visible emotion.

Often a director will score several of these points with a single movement, and in that moment the work becomes intensely theatrical. Sometimes the actor creates blocking, and sometimes only the director's outside eye can do the job. All blocking explicates text and ultimately theme. It is the play's visual score and counterpoint. Great directorial careers have been made by a singular talent for it. A director may have every other skill but, lacking this one, fails. When inadequate, few plays survive. Let's call it The Big Gorilla.

BLOCKING AS MEANING

Blocking becomes the external sign of the play's interior life. It is often a symbolic guide to the play's heart. Blocking also offers a continuing opportunity for the director and actor to discuss and adjust the meanings being made during this period. All choices made eliminate other possibilities, so reflection on the work done becomes an important part of the process. If you find yourself addressing blocking simply as a mechanical task, you lose its poetry and semantics. How is the blocking enhancing the understanding of story and character? If you can't understand the language, can you still follow events, character, and relationship through the play's physicality? We make meaning with space, with touch, with behavior, posture, and gesture. Every piece of blocking adds some layer of meaning to the production. In this sense, the blocking period tends to define the production far more than many directors even imagine. Blocking isn't just getting from here to there and back again. Blocking is also a language of heart and mind.

BEHAVIORAL BLOCKING

The simplest blocking of all. There's a full moon, and she goes to the window to see it. They've used up all the salsa, and he goes to the fridge for more. He didn't put a stamp on the letter to his brother, and he moves to the desk to do it. You get the point. These moves assist the story, provide physical variety, help the sense of reality, and anyone can figure them out. You can use them to solve simple spatial problems. She's been sitting too long; let's decide she's cold and crosses to the fire. Someone has to enter and not see the actor onstage. The entering actor has a bag of groceries, so he turns right into the kitchen and misses the actor left of the door who is straightening a painting. You have three people in a straight line; one moves down to an end table where she forgot her glasses. The behavior can be indicated by the stage directions or implicit in a line; or something you invent to solve a traffic problem. The idea is clear, he goes *there* to do *this*. Obviously, behavioral blocking stays inside the circumstances.

WHAT BEHAVIOR IS POSSIBLE?

The set model has been okayed. The floor has been taped for rehearsal. You've placed the furniture (designers have good ideas about this), checked the sight lines (the director, in the old days, would have a friend "walk" the stage for her), and sat in the rehearsal space alone imagining the play with this ground plan. Now think about the behavior. What can actors *do* on this set? Do you want practical lights to work with? Do the doors need locks? (Not real ones, please!) Do you want imaginary windows to open or close? Do you want a radio or TV to fiddle with? What can people do on that stairway? Are there walls and, if so, how will the actors relate to them? Where do the doors lead? If someone brings something on, where will they put it down? Is there a place for coats? Umbrellas? Do we need a flat space for writing? Will people lie down? Do you need some place to get someone higher than everybody else? In the final moment, what will the behavior be and where will it be? You haven't already done that, have you? You may not need all these behaviors but start out with enough.

PSYCHOLOGICAL BLOCKING

A mother misses her grown and gone son. She goes to his empty room, picks up his old catcher's mitt, and cradles it in her arms. (I know, I know, neither of us wants to see this play.) The immigrant has walked a thousand miles carrying his grandfather's rolled-up carpet. Now, in his new suburban house in Grand Rapids, he unrolls it on the floor and sleeps on it instead of on the bed. You get it. The character is compelled by past experience to use the current space in a particular way that reveals both character and text. If you're knowledgeable about the character's inside, you'd better block his outside. You can talk psychology and let the actor find the blocking or you can insist on blocking it and defend it psychologically. Either way the physicality is there to reveal a state of mind. This can, of course, dovetail with behavioral blocking and thus (oh joy!) achieve two things at once. Very often you understand a character's psychology more acutely after blocking is completed and thus need to revise the spatial work to include your recent insights.

BLOCKING AS SYMBOL
AND METAPHOR

Symbolism: "A method of expressing the invisible or intangible by means of visible or sensuous representation." Obviously, blocking can do that and thereby "reveals or suggests immaterial, ideal, or otherwise intangible truth or states." Blocking creates symbols that reveal theme, so it ain't just going for a Coke when you're thirsty. It coexists with and overlaps the behavioral. As to metaphor where "one idea or object is used in place of another to suggest a likeness or analogy between them." Lear is a sun with his power intact and a moon with it dispersed, and we could make images of giving and reflecting in our physical work. Physical relationships might signify dominance or submission. Postures adopted from early religious paintings might be used as metaphors of spiritual search in a contemporary play. Furniture and props can be used in this way. Try. Where you stand and how you stand can be assigned symbolic meaning. On the other hand, let's not overwhelm with these devices when unnecessary. Sometimes, a cigar is just a cigar. Are metaphor and symbol always meant to be understood by the audience? No. Sometimes it's a subliminal force. You can simply layer meanings. However, you need them in your toolbox. Reread the play you're doing and see what uses you can find for them.

BEAUTY AND COMPOSITION

Whether the blocking is behavioral, psychological, symbolic, or metaphoric, there is a concurrent level of finding forms that please the eye. The director's study of composition (moving and still) is a lifelong pursuit. Many of us begin by identifying the elements of composition in great paintings and great dance. Elements of composition include: the body and line of the actors in relationship to space, set, theater architecture, furniture, and each other. The director's trained eye works with spacing and juxtaposition of vertical and horizontal, the different planes and areas, high and low, straight line, triangle, and curve. The director works with how light carves space and reveals the body. The director makes use of patterns made by moving actors as well as the still frame and tableau. Composition uses repetition, stillness, movement, and surprise. To develop an aesthetic of movement you need, first, to become aware of the impact of the use of space and actor. Start *seeing* what you're doing as well as hearing it. The addition of a rhythmic sense to picturization will create an heady brew. View paintings, attend dance, study the landscape; whenever you like what you see, take a moment to ask why. There are wider worlds than behavior and psychology.

LAYERING

There's a big move. Twelve people on stage, seven have to pick up their spears and leave, two must remove a wounded man, and one must clean up all the broken glass before exiting. Meanwhile, downstage, our two leads are getting it on in a love scene. Layer the move a step at a time. Start, for instance, with the wounded man on the stretcher because that's likely to be an obstacle to other moves. With that set, add the guys who have to get their spears and leave. Have one go, then three, then two, then one (anyway, break their start times up to minimize sound distraction). Maybe by the time the last spear guy goes, the wounded man will be gone, and he can use the same exit. Now find a pattern for the woman cleaning up broken glass. You may have to run the spear guys' pattern several times to find her path. Now add any moves the love scene has. Okay, run the whole thing several times, making adjustments to protect the focus on the love scene. Run it again. Perhaps that's enough for now. You can make more adjustments tomorrow — layering, adding elements slowly to make it a whole.

EATING THE STAGE

Remember that 1970s rage for creating time exposure of headlights at night so you could see the entire path of the car in the photograph? Well, that's sort of what we're talking about here. The whole stage is pristine when the play begins, and the director should have used every inch of it by the time the lights go down for the last time. Eat the stage. As an audience member, I get fascinated by whole sections of the stage the director has seemingly abandoned. Why is it no person sets foot in that open space to the left of the door upstage? If she had no intention of using the love seat down left, why is it there? What about that space to sit on the stair landing? Is it contaminated? Often I find something has been saved for an important use later. Good. But never? It's like that character that keeps hanging around, semi-important but never making a real contribution. When you've finished rough-blocking the play, give yourself a quiet two hours to read through the script visualizing what's where and noticing any "where" that never got adopted.

SAVING A PLACE

So, we've blocked deep into the play and finally reached the blazing fight where our leading actress reveals her affair with her sister's husband and is stabbed before our very eyes. This definitely needs focus, needs to strike the audience, but where to play it? We've already played three scenes sitting in the two armchairs that face each other so that's used up. We played that other big scene at the dinner table. And, God knows, we've constantly used the window seat. What haven't we done? Sometimes this has to be our thought process, and sometimes we think ahead and save that damn window seat! We need strong looks to frame our important moments. Whenever possible we should have said to the designer, "What can we do that looks wonderful when the lovers finally get together in *As You Like It?*" Try to plan the big moment visually, don't just leave it to function in some overused area of the stage the audience is already bored with. That scene is the honored guest at the party. Save it a chair.

MOVEMENT AS ENTERTAINMENT

In the midst of talking about behavior and psychology and metaphor let's not forget the movement
the audience came to see! They came to see the big
dance at the Capulet party where Romeo and Juliet
meet. They came to see the swordfight, the acro-
batics, the villain swinging on the chandelier.
Where's the *theatrical* movement going to be in this
production? What's going to be fun to watch? This
applies to tragedy as well as to comedy, melodrama
and high romance. It even applies to (gasp!) realism.
In this latter form it may be the single moment when
Garth jumps over the sofa, or the cup gets thrown
against the wall, or Ellen hides the spinach she doesn't
like under the rug. Something, probably, that shat-
ters for an instant our idea of what should or could
be done in a living room. One whole play based on
theatrical movement was Meyers' *K2,* which had
mountain climbers climbing. On the other hand, the
simply magical moment of two people walking into
a kiss from across the room can seem amazing.
Sometimes the move is to delight and amaze.

THE ACTOR'S CONTRIBUTION TO BLOCKING

Small-cast realistic plays based on simple behaviors (life in the living room with lots of furniture) can be blocked decently while the director vacations in Bermuda. That's based on experienced actors. Empty the performance space of furniture and props and even a cast of three will need significant guidance. In that circumstance, only a few actors have the third eye that sees themselves in space. Once more actors are involved, it's hard for even the savvy performer to use the space sensibly inside the complex patterns without directorial help and editing.

Soooo, a rule of thumb would be, the smaller the cast and the more commonplace the behaviors the greater the actor contribution. More people, more space as metaphor, more complex behavior, the more the director *does* the blocking as opposed to the actor *finding* the blocking. Classics where a physical style is created need strong directorial guidance. In every situation the actors will bring ideas that should be respected and tried. The director should encourage contribution but retain the right to edit. Every blocking situation will be in some sense atypical.

REPEATING BLOCKING

Ordinarily you wouldn't do more than five pages before you went back and repeated the work. If it's a fairly straightforward section, one repetition should be sufficient before plunging on. If the blocking is complex and there are more than three or four people onstage, the repeat might come after three pages and two repetitions might help. If it's the lynching scene with fifteen people on stage and the kind of stage business where someone could be hurt, you might block only one page and then do several repetitions. There is no point in blocking long sections without this repetition. The blocking is the outside of rich interior lives helping deliver complex meanings from the text. You waste time by doing more than the actors can absorb and then having to redo it when no one remembers. On the third or fourth repetition of blocking the actors can shift their attention from the moves to acting inside them. I want to block a section, repeat it for memory, and then do enough directing inside the section to interest the actors in it and provide a strong basis for further work.

BLOCKING SCHEDULE

Obviously, there's no hard rule. However, plays are rehearsed in time, and scheduling time is a directorial talent. Some directors rough-block a play in three days and then spend the rest of rehearsal going back to add detail and revamp. I think it's a waste of three days and move more slowly, directing while I block. We must keep in mind that blocking is a delivery system for meaning, not a physical end in itself.

A rough rule of thumb is with three or fewer actors you may block four to five pages per hour. With three to six it may decline to three pages an hour, and with six or more you may get a single page done in sixty minutes. These are rough estimates depending on actor skills, director craft, and unusual demands of the material. When you stay on schedule, you don't waste people's time and you build confidence and trust. If you're an early career director, you may ask the stage manager to help keep track of your pace in the first day or two so you can use that knowledge in planning. A third of the rehearsal period (at least!) should be free for scene work and polishing after the blocking is complete. Spend effort on your schedule. You'll be praying for time in the last week.

BLOCKING AS PUNCTUATION

Gesture and blocking are, most often, punctuation to clarify text. So is sitting, standing, starting, stopping, entering, leaving, putting your Coke down, and slamming your book closed. Take sitting. Don't sit just anytime, sit to close an idea. The application of physical punctuation is of obvious value to directors. Movement starts when a sentence begins or ends. For one thing, a careful calibration of movement so that it doesn't distract from the sense of the line is crucial to understanding. Of course, any rules about blocking are made to be broken, but in this case less often than you might think. A sentence ends. An actress rises. She moves, speaking, across the stage. On the comma she picks up a book and continues her cross out the door and slams it simultaneously with the period. The structure of the line has been clarified, the necessary business completed, and a nice theatricality employed. The move can be psychologically apt, behaviorally revealing, even metaphoric, while protecting and explicating text.

BLOCKING AS
CHARACTER WORK

A wonderful actress, Adale O'Brien, whom I collaborated with for many years, used to say, "The good director gives you your character in the blocking." That blocking can access indecision, hyperactivity, fury, flirtation, alienation, you name it. You, by necessity, have to be thinking about the character's physicality, and you can't do that without thinking about character. An actor has to struggle to carve character when she hasn't been given the moves that allow it. Just as you can learn a great deal about character by watching a woman handle her dog, the audience learns by watching the character handle her prop. The director who approaches character through space and its uses is often the director who is intuitively theatrical. In each case, what are the physical clues that add up to our sense of personality? She touches, she doesn't touch. She's watchful, controlled. She can't sit still. She breaks personal space. She maintains distance. Don't forget these tools in the definition of character.

DEFENSIVE BLOCKING

Okay, let's hope actors don't read this book. Really good blocking hides the actor's weak points, and I'm not talking about his profile. Often in your career you'll be working a scene where one actor moves well and the other reminds you of the Frankenstein monster. It's your job to hide this problem. No matter what you had in mind (the tap dance is out), you have to deal with what you've got. Often you have to let the people who are at home on the stage dominate the movement. Stash the stiff in an armchair. If he's playing the lead (now aren't you sorry you let him audition sitting down?), sit him center. In the crowd scenes, create the sense of movement with the ones who are apt and use the others for pivots or stick them looking out of windows. The point is to change your original plan given the actors you have. I've seen directors commit artistic suicide by insisting on a physical idea the actors can't handle.

BLOCKING THE EMOTIONAL SCENE

Here you definitely have to let the actor's impulses into the process, and you damage those impulses if you tell her that she needs to cry, stand up, move weeping two steps left, yell "damn it!," pick up a book, and throw it so it lands on the sofa. One thing is clear, such a series of tasks insisted on too early will shut down what she is feeling. When the scene's emotion is high, try to incorporate the actor's impulses in the blocking. Later you can edit what seems out of balance. Shaping you can do.

"When you slide down the wall raging, could you do it another couple of feet to the left?" The actor will incorporate such change into the impulse fairly easily. Remember the actor isn't stage-managing this emotion (you hope). It has appeared because you and she have created circumstances and back story that produced the conditions where it could naturally appear, and now you want to make room for it inside your structure. If it comes down to faking the emotion (shhhh!), the director's role is different and we'll talk about that . . . privately.

DISAGREEMENT

The actor says, "That really doesn't feel right. I don't think she wants to be that close to him, and I don't think she would bring him a drink." Now what? How do you handle the moment? For a couple of reasons I usually request more information about the actor's feelings. I want more information to chew on. I want a second to get past any defensiveness I have. After they tell me their point of view (I hope fairly briefly) I ask what they would like to do instead, and we try that. Now it's up to the director to choose. If the actor's idea is better, say so and move on. If you want to insist on the original idea, fine, or you may now see a third way that could be tried. *Don't* give the actor any sense that he was wrong to have a thought! Even if you are under time pressure listen and decide. Another thing to remember is that if the actor *never* triumphs in discussion, it is likely to shut down his process, make him angry, or both. Sometimes I'll use the actor's idea even if I think it's second best (on behalf of the creative atmosphere), leave it for several days, and then come back and revise the sequence.

BLOCKING FOCUS

Blocking directs the eye and the ear. To do this you need to know what *needs* the focus. Your tools include:

1. Clever use (not overuse) of the strongest areas of your stage.
2. Someone starting to do something or stopping doing something.
3. Stillness.
4. The sudden move. The raised voice. The use of a prop. The sharp sound.
5. Everyone sitting still except one person moving. The reverse.
6. The composition leads your eye where it needs to go.
7. Emotion breaking through restraint. Restraint in the midst of emotion.
8. One person playing front.
9. Any surprise.
10. An entrance. An exit. A sit. A stand. Something new.

Blocking focus is a lifelong pursuit and each circumstance is singular. I find it helps enormously to know the moments you want to pop out of a scene. If you know *what,* you'll find how. Keep your eyes and ears open. Where should the focus go now? Now? Now? The actors, good ones, work on the same problem.

BLOCKING IN OPEN SPACE

There's a milky way painted on the stage floor, a starry sky above, and three actors alone on it without a chair, table, sofa, or drink cart in sight. How the hell do we block a two-hour play here? Obviously the changing physical relationships in the space reveal the changing emotional relationships in the text. The basics of this blocking include: the emotional need to move to relieve tension, the psychological need to be close to or far away from someone, the use of patterns (two people move in a clockwise and counterclockwise circle as conflict builds) and the paying of close attention to physical impulse.

Remember that physical punctuation can clarify text. Have an eye for the "beautiful" in the space. Don't be afraid to have people stand still (in an interesting composition) and talk. Use vertical planes as well as horizontal ones. One person standing, one person kneeling, one person lying, and such. Make good and significant use of the objects and furniture you do have (not overuse). Gesture means more and should be calibrated to mean more in such a space. Remember that austerity and rarity can fascinate, work slowly, don't panic.

SEEING AND USING THE ACTOR'S IMPULSE

You're blocking away and you notice the actor start to get out of the chair and sit back, waiting for your next instruction. If it's a good actor, he is probably having a good impulse. I'll either say, "Hey, I see you're wanting to get out of there, go ahead," or "Good idea but could you wait one more line until Jennie sits?" There are several reasons to grab and use the actor's impulse. First, you can't be tracking every moment of every character's psychology and you want help. Second, even if you later decide not to use that move you have shown respect for the actor's process and they will repay that in many ways. Third, it gets everybody trying things so you don't need to be the fountain head of every idea in the room. You can easily be so self-involved that they miss the tiny signals of impulse that the actor often restrains. Sometimes that impulse is the actor's desire to get back into a scene when you have been concentrating on others. Keep your eyes open and try to integrate these impulses into the work. It tells you the character is alive!

MOVING THEN STILL, STILL THEN MOVING

In the same way that silence gives sound impact (and vice versa), stillness gives focus to movement. The blocking you make sets the table for the moment the blocking stops. And what is that moment? Where is that moment? For heaven's sake, don't waste it. The stillness you create is there to reveal something important about the text. All right, the text resumes but still nothing and nobody moves. When the movement starts, it may be simple behavior, but that moment of starting should also make a textual point. I see plays where the still/moving equation seems random, pointless, and oblivious to text. I lay this wastefulness directly at the director's door. Think about how stillness is currently assisting in the telling of the tale in the script you're working on. We often say words are born in silence and we want the cross, the rise, the tango to have a similarly important beginning. Some directors are movement junkies and have no vocabulary of stillness, which gives their work ultimately a tinge of desperation. Use both, and decide when.

THE ARENA

I love staging in arena! There is no way the actor can play the house rather than her partner, because the audience is everywhere. Farce suffers in arena (as does Brecht) because not everyone sees both the set-up and the joke. Obviously long café scenes seated at a table are hard to manipulate ("You dropped your napkin. I'll come over and get it for you.") You do need to move people more and the actor needs to learn to "pan" key reactions (keep doing the reaction while turning slightly for better exposure to the audience), but blocking has a wonderfully three-dimensional feel. Remember that the entrances at the corners

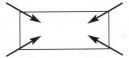

are a good strong place to stand because the most people can see your face. Knowing what's on the fourth wall and beyond is crucial for actor concentration, belief, and detail. The ground plan needs to be arranged to turn the actor every which way, and you need actors who like to move. Direct sitting on a different side of the rehearsal each day. Even so, once you get in the space, you'll notice the south side hasn't seen Helen's face in a long time. Warning: don't go too far and turn the actors into berserk lazy Susans. You can still stand still and play a two-minute scene.

ABANDONING CENTER

I recently saw a production (the audience sat on three sides) that had some twenty-five scenes, and I swear that eighty percent of that play, certainly every major speech, was played in about a four-foot square, dead center. You would have thought that space was magnetized. Sometimes the minor characters stood downstage of it, but the fear of changing the perspective was palpable. A physically varied use of the space assists in holding the audience's attention and makes and gives focus. The director overusing one area is like an actor forever using the same vocal pattern. The variety is more important than every moment being seen full front by every ticket buyer. Run through examining your use of the space to make sure that it's not repetitious. Think of space as a relationship between actors that is ever-changing and not always as a relationship between actor and audience.

I NEED TO GET YOU OUT OF HERE

Blocking is a time for directorial overload, and if there are more than three actors onstage you lose people in the process. You've left poor Joey on the sofa for several pages now and he's feeling stuck. To get him energized, active, and part of the scene you do in fact "need to get him out of there." I'll notice such a situation while I'm working with others and tell the actor, "I'll be with you in a minute." I'll give Joey parameters and let him solve the problem as in "why don't you move up behind the sofa sometime during this six-line section?" Joey likes the freedom and participates, usually finds a good moment, and you can keep working on the other side of the stage. You need to develop a keen sense of when the actor is feeling sidelined, boxed in, or finished with where they've been. An actor asks, "Haven't I been here too long?" and you need to invent behaviors that address his sense of being needlessly static. The actor is going to need to leave where he is sometime. When is that?

THE LONG MOVE
DOWNSTAGE OR UPSTAGE

This I love. My favorite blocking moment was when, on an open stage, the play's antagonist, defeated at last, crossed with her back to us from way downstage some eighty feet upstage and was finally swallowed up by the darkness. Yes! The same power is created by the reverse move all the way to the lip of the stage as exemplified by an endless opening cross down by Richard III. The long, long move.

Save such moves for the moments when they will deliver the most explosive meaning and deepest emotion. Any move over fifteen or twenty feet should be to make an impression. When I see the long move wasted on some commonplace behavior, I have a real, palpable sense of loss. You can build an entire play toward one of these downstage to upstage beauties. Is there an opportunity for one in the play you're currently rehearsing?

TOO MUCH BLOCKING

We all know directors who are blocking dervishes. Actors are in continual movement, back and forth they go. No sooner does one actor sit but another is off and running. They cross past each other and then back again. They lie down, stand on the stove, and are in and out of doors like greyhounds, and somehow it doesn't signify, doesn't reveal character or text; it's just busy. Either this director doesn't know the text well or fears it isn't interesting. And in the end that's just how it looks . . . as if the director were afraid.

After you've finished blocking, take a look at an early run through and ask yourself what can be cut away leaving meaning and interest intact? Can't they sit and talk a little longer? Does she really need all three trips to the kitchen? How much pacing does it take to tell us what we have to know? Often it becomes impossible to hear the script because it gets lost in the blocking. If you're unsure if what you're doing is too much, ask a veteran actor. She'll know.

MESSY

On a crucial level, the blocking is there to clarify the text, and at that moment of clarification, we don't want to be doing too many things at once. We don't want to be physically distracting. We don't want to be emotionally ornate. We don't need more lights, costumes, effects, activities. The blocking needs to be focused on making the point, no more and no less. Often things seem messy because the director doesn't seem to know what the point is (emotional, intellectual, or both) so everything going on seems inessential or messy. The blocking should focus on a key piece of dialogue, behavior, psychology, or story. Too much going on, too loud, too fussy, too self-consciously theatrical or comedic, too many gestures that don't punctuate text or reveal character, and the whole scene feels like an uncleaned room. Pare down to the essentials that make the point you want to make, otherwise the work is tainted by a kind of desperation that tips us off that the director isn't quite sure what needs to be going on. Clean focuses. Clean has a beginning, middle, and end. Clean makes the point the star.

TOO CLEAN

Sometimes there is a mechanical efficiency in the way the blocking is handled, in the ways the lines are delivered, and even in the actors' gestural vocabulary that seems devoid of spontaneity, real character, complexity, or life! Nobody ever seems indecisive, each gesture is clarified, each line has a key word, each posture seems contrived, and nothing, nothing surprises. It is, pardon the cruelty, like an open-casket viewing. At that moment insert a little vacillation, a little clumsiness, a tiny focus on the inessential (he finds a fly in his martini) a dollop of chaos in our overordered directorial universe. The craft, in other words, is too damn apparent! Not too much distraction, mind you, because we don't wish to obscure the essentials, but just enough to let a little air in. Sometimes we lose the sense of danger the live performance gives us. Leave a short sequence open to nightly improvisation. Ask the actor if she has an instinct to do something you haven't examined. Careful though.

THE INTERMEDIATE MOVE

All right, four lines from now Bob's going to faint and Helen, his wife of twenty years, will say "Oh my God, Bob!" and go to his aid. Right now they are both on the sofa. If he faints there, he will slump over and then she will lean forward, run her hand through his hair, and say you know what. Surely we need something a little more dramatic! Getting that will involve *intermediate* moves. Hmmm. How about Bob sees the ceiling is peeling from an apparent water leak and stands up to get a better look. Helen, getting the point, heads for the front door to get the stepladder. He now crashes to the floor from his upright position, and she races to his fallen form screaming . . . well . . . that line. The director, chess player that she is, needs to think more than one move ahead. Many pieces of blocking, though motivated, are simply preparations for what is to come. This implies knowing the script well enough to begin physical preparations even pages ahead.

THE "COUNTER"

Now here's an old traditional move you need to master. When actor A moves down to talk to actor B, actor C, who was talking to A, finds a reason to move away as A approaches B. And now, a second confusing example: several people are onstage, enough to cause traffic problems. One actor has moved between the couch and chair to overhear someone's conversation. Another actor needs to cross between the couch and chair to exit. As the exiting actor starts for the door, the actor blocking the path just happens to remember he left his drink stage left and "counters."

Sometimes the counter is someone consciously moving out of the way, and sometimes it needs an entirely different reason. With experienced actors you say, "Jack, when he starts that cross will you counter," and the actor figures out why and to where. Sometimes the countering actor goes where another actor can shortly cross to her. The counter not only clears for a current piece of blocking but sets up the next one. Usually, but not always, the counter is the job of an actor not speaking.

THE ANGLE

Need I say we're talking about:

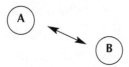

When we use the term *flat* we mean:

For some reason when the two actors are on an angle the stage looks dynamic and when they are flat it seems boring. The angle when used in blocking is constantly shifting and reforming. So far we've been talking about a look with one actor at the top of the angle and the other at the bottom, but the angle is also powerful as a blocking move as in:

If you are conscious of using the angle as a relationship between actors and as a path for a single actor, you will find endless permutations. Personally I prefer almost any angle to flat. Why? Because.

THE TRIANGLE

There are a couple of shapes in blocking that have a lot of energy and intrinsic beauty.

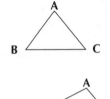

or

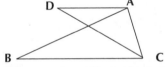

or any of the possible versions. You can also add people.

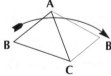

Very often we move from one triangle to another as in:

In arena staging and in three-quarter it turns out to be the dominant staging shape. (Yes, I know, not in two-character plays.) You may want to make the triangle possible in your ground plan. Why it works so well, looks so good, and feels so dynamic is one of those mysteries of the stage. It seems to have good psychology and good aesthetics. Use some.

THE MULTIPLE MOVE

First he crosses. He stops. Now she goes to turn on the lamp. Literally *one* move after another. Too many single moves and the viewers suffer terminal boredom. The eye needs a certain complexity. How about two people going opposite directions at the same time.

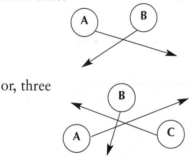

or, three

Pick your own combination. He sits down *as* she's getting up. Look for a few multiple simultaneous moves. Maybe the speaker is the one standing still to protect the language. Or the speaker moves center or down center to keep the focus. Or pair a curve and a straight line

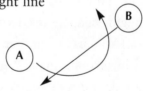

I've seen entire plays done one move at a time. Give our eyes a break.

THE LAG

Next play you see, watch for the following. The majority of the time only the speaker moves. This is a primitive way of controlling the focus. If the person listening is always still, it assures that the speaker's punctuation of the line with movement controls our focus on the line. A good idea as far as it goes, but overused, it gives a mechanical and predictable look to the proceedings. The lag means that the person who has finished speaking continues a move during the next person's line.

In many scenes the text centers on actor A while B and C ask questions or provide secondary information. In this case we want to maintain focus on A, and she can safely move while others speak. A reversal of this idea in a group scene leaves A still and powerfully positioned while several others move simultaneously. The point is that movement and text are steadily manipulated by the director to provide focus and variety simultaneously. The lag is one way to break the pattern of "speaker moves."

GROUPS

Some day (but not very often in the American theater) you're going to have thirty people on stage. Perhaps it's *Cyrano* or you're doing your first opera.
In this sort of scene six people talk and the rest
watch, cheer, work, flirt. Visually it often helps to
break the supernumeraries into groups. Let's say
they range from groups of three to seven (odd numbers are visually helpful). Each group has a subject
of conversation and/or an activity. It also just so happens that each group is a visual composition the eye
enjoys. Is this old-fashioned? Yes, but it works when
time is of the essence. Somewhere amidst all this the
principal actors are playing a scene. If it's a prosce-
nium stage, the scene is probably downstage of the
groups. In arena you would have levels to work
with. While the scene progresses, the groups appear
fluid but not intrusive. An actor from group A
moves to group C, etc. Each time a new composition is created. These groups need to understand the
circumstances of the scene they are playing. If asked
to react to dialogue they will first react within the
group. Sometimes a group is busy within itself.
Sometimes it focuses on the action for a time. Careful planning is essential. The director may need to
storyboard.

OTHER CROWD TIPS

We've talked about groups and their uses, and here are a few more ideas. First, the crowd's work is based in the circumstances of the scene, so make sure they hear and understand them.

1. Exits and entrances for crowd members. Do they all have to be there all the time?

2. For crowd behavior you probably need props. Make a list of usable stuff for the crowd. Don't overdo it.

3. Have five-minute meetings with each participant. Give each a character touch, a behavior, and a sense of how she contributes to the point of the scene.

4. Individualize one crowd member by the way he relates to a principal at a key moment.

5. Families are always a good group basis. Also age- and sex-specific groups.

6. Make crowd reactions specific down to writing dialogue for individuals and groups.

7. Make sure you have planned sufficient rehearsal time to do specific work.

8. You'll get better work done and greater commitment if you take the time to learn their names.

9. Work for unobtrusive flow. Don't have everyone standing about.

THE DIRECTOR, THE STAGE MANAGER, THE BLOCKING

Okay, so you're blocking a crowd scene in *Three Musketeers*. You're a demon, you're possessed, you're fast, hell, you are blocking a mile a minute! Meanwhile, your admirable stage manager — the tortoise to your hare — is cramping as she tries to get this great stuff written down. Hold up there, pardner, have a little mercy. Remember that tomorrow when Actress X has no idea whether to cross right, left, or sit, and you certainly don't remember, you will turn desperately to this same stage manager for help, and she won't be able to help because you showed her no consideration the day before. When blocking big or complex scenes, check in with the stage manager. If she is falling behind, you may need to stop blocking, take a five, or go back and review what you've done a couple of times with the cast until she has caught up. This is both common courtesy and common sense. Boy, will it save you trouble later.

Working with
the Actor

THE ACTOR WANTS

1. To understand where the director is taking the play and how that director sees the character.

2. You to have done your directorial homework.

3. You to know the story and its circumstances.

4. A supportive creative atmosphere that encourages risk and rewards participation.

5. To make a contribution to the process, to have ideas and have them heard.

6. The play will to blocked expeditiously.

7. To feel comfortable about coming to you with a problem.

8. The work done in an atmosphere of mutual respect.

9. You to control the room in a positive way so that group process is possible.

10. To know that you will not give up on her.

11. You to give clear, practical, and stimulating notes.

12. You to be a problem solver and handle people well.

13. You to notice when she does something right.

14. To respect you.

15. You to make it better.

TAPE

This is what I call the delivery of lines by actors who have previously decided exactly how they will read them, emphasis, intonation, and all. As a director you need to be sensitive to this phenomenon in auditions, rehearsal, and performance. Yes, of course, some degree of this is found in every performance, but not whole scenes, not whole acts! The casualty of this kind of acting is interplay between the actors ,and where there is no interplay, the work lies there like a dead fish. Much of this sort of work happens because the actor is afraid. "I only have this one idea" he thinks, "I mustn't let go of it." The director can deal with this problem by reemphasizing the circumstances of the scene (or even changing them) so the actor's reading no longer serves. Sometimes there is no substitute for being frank and saying "Could you change that reading, it's getting stale?" All the acting should stay within the circumstances, but that is possible with a constant small variety of readings.

POINTING OUT THE
ACTING TRAPS

In every role there are built in acting traps that can hobble performance. A constant melancholy tone in *Hamlet*. Too much shouting in *Lear*. Too depressive in *Hedda*. Trying too hard to be funny as Harlequin. Working at Lenny's dimwittedness. The prepared director has thought about the traps for any part of size in the text (too angry too long applies to a thousand roles). When is the time to discuss this with the actor? Early. At the table or early in the blocking. I talk to an actor about the traps quietly to one side, on the break or over a beer. The actor appreciates this kind of tip from you because it's a relief not to make those mistakes in the public arena of rehearsal. Often the actor falls into a trap you had not foreseen, such as giving the part so much business that important lines are being lost. Try to communicate these traps early so that the actor doesn't set negative patterns or become too fond of her choices. Believe me, you need to cut such patterns off at the pass.

RESPECTING THE ACTOR'S TIME

Professional actors work a six-day week, and they are always struggling to find time for their personal life and necessary tasks. If you want the actor's admiration and a cast with strong morale, treat their time with respect. Start rehearsals and end rehearsals on time. Give five-minute breaks on the hour. More important, don't call actors in and then make them sit and wait. Schedule and stick to it. When you run late on a scene, walk out and apologize to the actors who are waiting. If it's still going to be some time before you use them, release the actors for an hour or two. Directors who call actors in on the off chance they may use them accumulate bad will. In run-throughs if the actor is only in the second act, give her a later call. A less obvious cause of bad will is the director who has run out of work he wants to do and fills the time with too many run-throughs. In an emotionally demanding play it is exhausting for the performer, makes repetitive labor out of creativity, and sours the atmosphere.

WHY?

The actor is, sensibly, interested in the rehearsal process. Before beginning work for the fifth time on a scene, it behooves the director to say what is being worked *on*. If a scene is being reblocked or cut, you will have better buy-in if you tell the actors why. If you have done your work at all well, the actors believe themselves to be not only your creative partners but intelligent contributors skilled enough to solve problems. If the director makes himself the one who is going to solve problems only he can understand, the actor is naturally suspicious and even paranoid. He is likely to think that what is being worked on is his fault but you don't even have the confidence in him to say so. Early career directors tend to believe that it is their responsibility to fight creative battles alone and that certain information is best kept from the actor. Wrong. It takes the village. The more of your thought process that is vouchsafed the actor, the more minds and skills will assist you with it. The worker appreciates and is energized by the reasons for the work.

THE EMOTION

You can talk about the scene in a way that opens up the impact of the situation on the characters. You can heighten the circumstances and hope the emotion will be engaged. You can personalize moments in the play by using your own life as an example and hoping it reminds them to use theirs. You can emphasize the relationships, which is where the trigger for emotion exists. You can make sure the blocking makes use of their impulses and allows a physicality that can release emotions. You can assist them in finding the right time in the text to abandon restraint, to go full out. You can make sure they are fully contacting the other actor whose actions will produce emotion. You can raise the stakes and encourage them to battle the obstacle so that the losses the character incurs are deeply felt. You cannot ask for the emotion by name. You can only create and heighten the circumstances that may catch lightning in the bottle. The emotions are the actor's province. You can only woo them.

ANCILLARY ACTION

Simple tasks are a wonderful directorial device. When the actor is having a hard time making sense of the big speech or seems self-conscious trying to play the scene just standing there, ask her to tie her shoe, get a splinter out of her hand, or put on some eye shadow. An amazing transformation takes place. The speech or scene is alive and concentrated. Where there seemed no real thought process, one appears magically. Instead of trying to fake "Oh, what a rogue and peasant slave am I," the speech becomes real, punctuated, and believable. Sometimes we don't know how or what to act, but we always know how to tie our shoe or sand a chair. These ancillary actions may even be a transitory device that can be removed later when the actor is more comfortable. They are of particular use with talented but inexperienced actors. When the work in front of you seems uncomfortable or false, try grounding it with a simple, clear task that has a definite endpoint.

VACILLATION

In life we start for the kitchen, go five steps, notice we've forgotten our empty glass, go back, start again, stop for an instant to check our watch, go to the kitchen door, look back to see if you've put the cheese tray out, and exit. Too often this natural vacillation is left out of the blocking process. Remember, in life there are few straight lines in our physical behavior. These sorts of vacillation do not relate to the long cross. We also want the moments where someone starts to rise from the sofa, decides not to, starts to rise again, still feels it's wrong, and then gets up. It is these vacillations during the physical work that imply the actor's thought process, so we don't get the blocking score that implies the actors only think when they are still. You often have to remind an actor of the values of vacillation and sometimes and have to build it into the blocking. Watch for its absence in your own work so you can layer it in. It gives fabulous texture.

TRYING THE ACTOR'S WAY

Always, always try the actor's suggestion. And having done so, be complimentary if you adopt it. If, having tried it, you don't believe it fills the bill, say so. You want to involve the actors in making the play and that won't happen if you insist all the ideas be yours. If the actor involvement seems low, ask them which of two ideas you have seems the best? Even if you know exactly what to do (when the actor should leave the sofa and cross left) it's sometimes best to leave the decisions to the actor. You must create a fertile situation where ideas flow from several sources. A good idea makes you look good wherever it came from. If the actors are standing around waiting to be told what to do, something in your manner has created that situation. The actors look for signals from the director as to how much participation in the creative process will be appreciated.

TALKING WITH,
NOT TALKING AT

You need to be able to tell the difference. An actor talking *with* creates a sense of truth, provokes reaction, deepens the audience's interest, and plays with greater variety. The actor talking *at* is playing alone, leaves the other actor in a spot; she seems stagier and less attractive. Now there are people in life who "talk at," so, yes, it could be a character trait, but it's an unpleasant one, so make sure that's useful. Talking at is usually a sign that the actor is not playing an action but is simply demonstrating the text. Focus the actor on the action and see if that helps. The actor talking *at* is aware of the other person's reaction and thus isn't adjusting for it. Force this actor to take in what the other person is doing and change her tactic. Unfortunately, a great many actors who don't really engage and a great many directors can't tell the difference. You will not always succeed in getting an actor to engage. Pick the moments when it is crucial and work on those until you get results. Learn to hear and see this problem.

DIRECTING THE MUSICAL ACTOR

Good actor-singer-dancers are like the proverbial needle in the haystack and when you find them, you can't afford them. Singer-actors? Possible. Dancer-actors, don't ask. Anyway, you're directing this musical, now what? Sometimes it's all miked, sometimes only the numbers. The bottom line in musical acting is that it needs tremendous energy in the book scenes to compete with the sound and energy of the numbers.

Good musical actors know this and deliver high energy, which cuts down a bit on variety and detail. They are used to big auditoriums (because of the economics) and tend to work louder, faster, and move more (to fill the space). Little relationship touches can be lost so they tend to play front more. They are often directed by choreographers who have less interest in the book scenes. My advice is that if you understand the energy needs, you can add more acting and relationship details than ordinary and the cast will love you for it. Musical actors adore the rare director who really invests in the book. Clarify terms, give confidence in subtler work, but remember, they know their craft.

HANDLING LANGUAGE

A big subject in a small space. The actor has her mind, her emotions, her body, her face, the surround, and the words. Here are a few common mistakes in dealing with text.

1. The actor isn't using, relishing, filling, emphasizing, or enjoying the words.
2. The actor isn't paying attention to the punctuation and understanding suffers.
3. He's breaking up the sentence so much you can't follow it.
4. She's misreading the line and screwing up the emphasis. Yes, you may have to tell her.
5. The most important information is often at the end of the line, and that's where they run out of vocal energy.
6. Equal emphasis, so we can't crack the meaning.
7. Low energy and low stakes. If the speaker isn't passionate about what he is saying, why should we be?
8. The actor is interested in tone and attitude. It isn't clear what she's saying and how it affects the situation.
9. If we can't hear it, it doesn't matter what you do with it.
10. You need to relate this sentence to the sentence two lines earlier.

Directors often maintain a hands-off policy toward language. Mistake. It's there to reveal plot and character and so are you. Pick up the cudgel.

THE BIG SPEECH

These are the ones the actors die to do. These are the ones the audience remembers. In Shakespeare it's the soliloquy that informs, foreshadows, or presents the character figuring out what the hell to do. In contemporary drama, it's the fulcrum moment where the past informs the present and the play's course is defined or altered. The key to all these speeches is to remember that no matter how seductive they are, they're not ends in themselves. If it's reliving the past ("I once saw Michael Jackson in a Kmart.") and other characters are onstage, help the actor find what the hidden message in the memory is. What's the present action in the nostalgic speech? What is he really saying to his wife with the Michael Jackson story? We need to embed the big speech in the forward movement of the play. Don't let it stop the story like a huge rock in the road. Like the well-designed song in the musical, it should deepen relationships, move the story, and force others to react. Make the actor doing these speeches make somebody else do something. These speeches need to be incitements, not simple declarations. Don't keep the big speech trapped in a glass jar, make it reach out.

GETTING THE ACTOR
TO THINK

When the actor isn't living inside the text or reacting to the circumstances and is blundering through
the transitions and simply parroting words, words,
words, what then? You need to lobby for a thought
process. Say:

1. What are the key circumstances that surround
   this scene and moment?

2. What do you want the other person to do?

3. What's the obstacle to getting what you want?

4. What two things are you deciding between at
   this moment?

5. What's the most important part of the speech?

6. How does this moment relate to the moment in
   the first act when he says . . .

7. I need to see you choose the words.

8. The speech is flat, it all sounds the same.

9. The moment's stale, read it differently.

10. Could you put a quick part (or slow part) in that
    speech?

11. What are you getting from her now?

12. Put a couple of one-beat pauses in the speech.
    "Where?" Wherever you want.

You invent another dozen.

GETTING THE BODY
INTO THE SCENE

All too often the actor seems like a statue with moving lips. We could divide the world of actors into those whose mind and emotion continually show in the body, and those whose nervous system and blood flow seem to have stopped dead at the neck. Sometimes reminding the actor that they need to get their body into the scene helps. Sometimes you need to provide behavior, a prop, an ancillary action ("Tie your shoe while you talk") or, God help us, say "At the door look at Jane then reach for the book, decide you don't need it, and brush the crumbs off your sweater."

That's right, you may have to block simple physical events that make the actor look alive. Yes, the body usually reacts to a strong action, a strong obstacle, and high stakes but some actors stop living when they hit the stage. Make sure you are seeing this lack of physical detail and find a way to attack it. Stillness? You bet. But stillness is a product of deep concentration or imminent decision or a gathering of forces. Are you seeing stillness or absence?

LETTING IT LAND

Letting it land means allowing us to see the impact on one actor of what the other actor says or does. Sometimes it's one actor becoming aware of their own thoughts and actions. Letting it land creates a space where things can be reviewed, chewed, and understood. Some people call it taking the arrow, some people call it reacting, some people just call it taking time. Sometimes pace sweeps along at such a rate that there's no room to react to good news, bad news, or any news at all. Often the director has to build such moments in, or even suggest that a reaction is needed or, God help us, say what the reaction might be. So, make time for the actors to process the key stimulus. Give confidence that such moments are not only stageworthy but theatrical. This is an area where the actor needs encouragement and gentle urging. As always the questions remain, let what land when? The director's sense of the important moment that strikes home is the map for the use of the tool. Without that, the abyss.

ON THE LINE/
OFF THE LINE

Here's the mother of all generalizations: In contemporary plays you can act *off* the line and in verse or pre-Freudian plays you do the vast majority of the acting *on* the line. In other words, off the line means acting in the pauses, after the periods, any silence you can find. On the line means just what it says, you do the thinking and self-reacting while you talk. "Joan," you'll say, "You're breaking up the line so often I can't remember what it's about. You need to act more on the line." Conversely you may say, "Benny, the part is flying by as if you didn't own a thought process. For God's sake, do a little acting off the line." Once the actors understand your vocabulary, you can get results that might have taken you hours of line-by-line examination. Warning: Any such generalizations about how to handle text will be confounded by specifics in any rehearsal period. Nevertheless . . .

GOING SLOWER

For some actors, speed is addictive. It gives them the illusion of spontaneity because at a certain tempo they feel the thrill of being out of control. Plus you don't have to know too much about the text, you just have to rattle it off. Slower creates air in the text, gives more room to savor and consider moments, allows more moments to land. If you force the actors to take time, you will immediately see what content they have to give, and when there isn't much, you'll know the scene needs further examination. Another problem with overpacing is that it gives no space for the emotions to bloom. The overpaced play tends to seem intellectual and heady. Sometimes it isn't the scene but a single actor who needs to be pulled back. Don't be afraid to use slower as one of your tools. Sometimes the result will be miraculous. An actor you've mentally written off becomes fascinating to watch in an instant. What is, of course, needed is a variety of tempos, but slower can open the door to a richer scene.

TAKING NOTES/
GIVING NOTES

Any way you take notes is flawed. If you write them,
you have to look away from the stage. If you use a
note taker, it's distracting to the actor. If you record
them, it's a pain to transcribe them. Choose your
poison. I write in pencil on legal pads averaging forty
to fifty notes per act. Many are reminders to work
small or large sections, and the actors never hear
them. Many are marked (T) for tech notes. If the
note is for a specific actor, I start with the character's initials. When you give notes, be specific. Whenever possible it should relate to a line or brief section.
If you have general feelings about a role or scene,
it probably needs a working session, not a note. It
is often key as to when and how you give the note.
If the actor is upset and has had a bad day, you may
want to hold certain notes till tomorrow. Don't get
into long discussions over a single note while the rest
of the cast sits idle; see the actor later. Don't allow
your personal frustration with the actor to color the
note or the way you give it. Try in giving the note
to concentrate on the problem not the actor. The
actor relates better if the implication is that he is
capable of doing the fix. In addition to content,
notes are a matter of charm, diplomacy, and timing.

THE INADEQUATE ACTOR

You cast her. She's inadequate. Remember *you* cast her. Now what? If you're going to replace her, do it soon. Don't let it drag on. If you're going to keep her, see if the following helps:

1. Spend time alone with the actor.

2. Be specific about the role's requirements. No big words. The real deal.

3. Repetition. Repetition. Repetition.

4. Work small segments with this actor. Don't leave them until she improves.

5. Trim lines. Cut sections. If the actor can't move, simplify the blocking.

6. In this actor's scenes, give more focus to the other actors.

7. Give him simple activities to do while he speaks.

8. Do props help?

9. If there is something she does well have her do more of it.

10. Force him to play an action.

11. Keep after her about raising the stakes.

12. Sit him down. If he can't move, maybe he can talk.

13. At least try to fix the key moments. Prioritize.

14. Stop her from doing the things you can't stand.

15. Remain calm and civil. If he does something right, make much of it.

GO BACK TO THE GIVENS

A scene isn't working, or it has ceased to work. Review, first for yourself and then for the actors, the given circumstances of the scene and the relationships. Somewhere in those circumstances is a condition you must be missing. You can do this by going back to the table or on your feet with the actors. I say, "What given circumstances are important to us now?" Many times it is one of the actors who comes up with the one we're missing or have forgotten. The same technique can break open a single moment. Every moment in a play is governed by elements of the situation. Have you forgotten the time pressure? Have you forgotten what each of the characters has to lose? Have you overlooked someone's physical state? Is it clear what each person still needs from the relationship? If (as I hope) you have made a list of given circumstances before you went into rehearsal, you should be reviewing it often (and adding to it). There's almost always an answer to your problems in that list.

BUILDING RHYTHM

You will work with actors who are rhythmically challenged. Their rhythm is as steady as rain on the roof. You ask them to vary their speech and body rhythms; they say yes and then they don't. What then? Roll up your sleeves and build the rhythm yourself. "The first three lines need to be quick and stacatto, then a four-second pause while he decides, then she takes her time responding. Then the rest of the scene goes at machine-gun speed." Really? You can be that specific with actors? Yes, when time's limited. The audience's attention is drawn to the moment where the rhythm changes. The moment of change gives focus. After a certain point, steady rhythm lulls. Obviously you don't focus on rhythm to the exclusion of sense and circumstance. Some actors have as finely tuned and instinctive a sense of rhythm as any blues singer — and some don't. Take an hour and listen to the play as it's evolving. When your ear is sensitized, it's amazing what you'll become aware of rhythmically, and what needs doing.

LET ME TELL YOU WHAT
I'M GETTING

Here's a phrase worth its weight in gold. The actors clearly understand that they have limited objectivity and they accept (sometimes grudgingly) the director as a necessary outside eye. When an actor is headstrong or defensive about a choice, it is usually definitive to use the phrase above. When you tell the actor what you are receiving from what they are doing, he will often be amazed. "But that's not in the least what I intended," he'll say. At that point you achieve control of the moment in question. "No, I'm sure you don't intend it, but to get what you're after, we'll need to go about it a little differently." The ball is now in your court and the actor will (usually) try the adjustment you suggest. You must tell the actor clearly what you are receiving; don't exaggerate. Most important, never use this phrase unless you have a useful remedy for the actor that assists him in changing what he's doing.

CRITICIZING ONE ACTOR
TO ANOTHER

Here's a pitfall I've fallen into it, and probably so have you. It usually happens this way: An actor you like, respect, and have worked with before tosses out a quick criticism of another actor as if you were already in agreement. Don't take the bait. You can't afford to take general sides in the rehearsal process. If you do, it often sets up a dynamic where the criticized actor is always "wrong." Additionally, actors are sensitive to being ganged up on and either shut down or become defensive enough to cause a full-scale war. Sometimes actor A will baldly ask you to stop actor B from doing something. The best thing to say is that you hear them and will keep an eye on the moment or scene in question. Actor A will be wrong as often as she is right. In rare cases you may have to address the problem straight on and say you would prefer she didn't criticize the other actor because it puts you in an awkward position.

KEY MISTAKES THE ACTOR
MAY BE MAKING

1. He isn't playing an action.

2. She's playing the action but working an insufficient obstacle so there is no tension.

3. He's talking at, not with, the other actor.

4. She's completely forgotten the super objective.

5. He's playing all in one tone.

6. She's playing all in one rhythm.

7. He's playing the action but not varying the tactics.

8. She's are playing with low stakes.

9. He needs something to do.

10. She's not getting any body into the part.

11. He's playing one thing too long.

12. She's acting tone or making atmosphere instead of playing what she wants.

13. He's not really interested in the role he's playing.

14. She's not filling the words with meaning.

15. He hasn't personalized the part.

DOWN TO THE LAST BLINK

Now listen here, everyone who directs prefers to believe that the main job is to stimulate and edit rather than to insist on every detail. But there are times. I recently directed a large musical and a crucial dancing role had two short, important dialogue scenes. The dancer playing the role confided to me at the first rehearsal that he had never spoken on stage before. In this case I "made" the performance on him in the same way a choreographer "makes" the dance on a dancer. Every moment, every turn, every gesture, every touch, even every look-away and look-back. Had some essential rule of the director/actor relationship been horribly broached? No. In the end any means (short of physical danger or emotional harassment) can be justified by the quality of the result. These cases are rare, but young directors are hesitant to make the moment on the actor even when there is no other way to achieve it. This is not an everyday occurrence, but when there is no other way, don't hesitate.

DEALING WITH THE
DERANGED INTELLECTUAL

Theater is filled with smart people. There are some extraordinarily smart people. Many of these people will be actors in your plays. Some of these smart people use their fecund minds to avoid rehearsing the play. These people will be in your play also, so we probably need to talk about them for a minute. Please remember that most (I won't say all) conversations in rehearsal are meant to relate directly to some part of the text. The long conversation about what the Stoics believe should, within a reasonable time, result in some visible or audible change or enhancement in how the text is being played. Be careful that you aren't led down the garden path of engaging in debate rather than directing the play. One thing we can all agree about directing is that your time is both precious and short. To be fair to all parties, some directors who engage in the same ploy, are smarter than they are skilled. Three minutes is a long time in rehearsal, five minutes is forever, and ten minutes is eternity. Others are waiting. Talk needs to lead to action.

GIVING UP ON AN ACTOR

Here's a directorial sin. Beware. Of all the people you wouldn't want to be trapped in a room with, you'll doubtless get to direct several. Sometimes an actor may be so resistant or so dense or so time-consuming or so angry that you just check out and direct the pliable, open, cheerful, and talented souls. It's so much easier, right? Here's where you have to have the proverbial true grit. You can switch your focus away from the difficult person for fifteen minutes to regain your calm or even for a day if you are truly at your wit's end, but you must rejoin the fray. I've had a couple of knockdown, drag-out tiffs with actors I never thought I could direct again, but your responsibility to the play and the rest of the team takes precedence. Try a peace offering, or a coffee date, or revise your vocabulary concerning the role. Try positive notes or more time on the stricken scene. Some actors don't want you to direct them and have an arsenal to achieve that end. Never give up, never give in. Onward.

COMPLIMENTS

Some directors don't like to give them for fear the actors will stop working. I think they are a crucial part of the rehearsal process. Very often I'll offer them on the way to the Coke machine on a five-minute break. "Damn," I'll say as I pass. "You're going to be funny in this part!" or "This part is right down your alley" or "That's going so much better" or "That last moment broke my heart." Every actor has a nagging fear that what he is doing won't work and he'll be ridden out of town on a rail. Sometimes a little confidence and support will diminish the fear and allow a breakthrough. I'm not suggesting you give a compliment you don't mean, but sometimes it can be given to good effect before the accomplishment is complete. Who would you rather take risks for, the director who believes in and admires you or the one who only gives negative notes? The idea that you can scare and bully actors into good work is a mistaken and counterproductive one.

THE WORKHORSE

I remember directing a veteran actor in a Miller play who took me aside and said, "Listen, somebody has to drive this play." He meant someone had to apply constant pressure on the situation. You will find yourself in casts where most of the actors are by nature reactive. They like to sit back and react to other actors' initiatives. There's trouble. You must single out an actor with the role and lines to drive the play and push her to be more aggressive. Steadily more aggressive. You also need to be aware in the casting process to put actors who have sufficient acting energy and an instinct for the scene's jugular in the parts that drive the plots. Often these roles are not the play's showiest. These are Dr. Watson parts, not Sherlock Holmes. The point is that someone needs to carry the energy load and often he will need encouragement from you. Whose job is it in the scene?

LOW ENERGY

Confession. For years I had a taste for actors who give richly detailed performances, highly reactive but small in scale, and not aggressive. And did I ever get burned! Energy, the crucial acting ingredient. The common wisdom is that you can pull an actor down but you can't pump her up. True. Please, please make sure the actor has the energy to deliver the role before casting her.

But now you've made the mistake, what can be done? You can help, but in a large role you probably can't fix. You tell the actor the energy is low, but the low-energy actor can't truly recognize it. Get her to raise her stakes in the situation. Tell her whatever she wants to want it more. The problem is she may advance today but regress tomorrow. You may need to do an unusual number of repetitions to make the progress stick. Demanding energy puts these actors at levels of strain that has an unpleasant and flat quality. Try working for short bursts of high energy for specific beats and actions. Try to have other actors carry the scene's energy load. Pray. Dance. The moral to this story is to take the extra time in auditions to make sure the actor has the life force to carry a major role.

TOO HIGH/TOO LONG

There are actors tuned like racehorses, so high-spirited and energetic that they constantly explode with energy. There are actors who love to rage and shout. There are actors whose bodies are always in motion. Anything sustained too long (but particularly the loud and the busy) grates. The director has a couple of options. The first is to tell the actor just what there's too much of and assume he will solve it. The second is to insert moments that break the actor's momentum. If, for instance, the problem is volume, insert a fairly long pause that breaks the actor's forward thrust. If it's continual physical movement, sit him down or tell him to put his hands in his pockets. Some directors have too high a tolerance for a high decibel level, but even they can identify a lack of variety. Don't let the actors set this kind of pattern because once they get attached to it, it's hard to break. Too high, too long can pull the audience out of the play.

THE ATTENTION SPONGE

You recognize this situation. Every time you turn around the same actor is at your elbow saying, "Was that any better?" or "I'm missing something in the scene with Joe, what is it?" After rehearsal you hear the patter of little feet and then the questions seeking reassurance start again. This is harmless, right? Depends. If it gets on your nerves or blackens your mood, it's not good for your morale and your morale is important. It may also turn the cast against the actor both out of embarrassment and the feeling that this person is getting more than her fair share of your time. In this circumstance if this obsessive behavior continues, it's best to have a private conversation. Say, smiling, that the work is coming along nicely, she has no significant problems, but she needs too much reassurance. Yes, just like that, bluntly but not meanly. She'll stop.

ACTOR VS ACTOR

This is, I think, my least favorite actor problem. One actor complains to you about the work of another. Usually it has to do with the complaining actor's feeling that she's "not getting what she needs," or "he's killing my laughs" or "he doesn't know her lines" or "he's hurting me." The problem for you is that once you obviously take sides in the dispute, you lose respect from both actors. Another problem is that the complaint may have merit. What to do? Look directly at the complaining actor and say, "Thank you, I'll consider the problem," and no more. If the actor continues in the same vein, say, "I'd prefer not to talk anymore about this at this time." If necessary move away at this point. Having responded, watch to see if there is a problem. If you decide there is, speak to the offending actor privately, but base your comments on *your* perception, not the actor's complaint. Having done so, tell the actor who complained (also privately) that the issue is closed.

USING THE OBSTACLE

The obstacle is what prevents the actor from easily achieving the action. If Juliet and Romeo weren't from warring families, the balcony scene would be just another date. The obstacles are what create the tension and drama. When the director senses that the scene is lying there like a dead elk, she should compare the actor's current sense of the obstacle to his needs and wants. Perhaps the obstacle needs to be toughened or heightened. Try articulating the obstacle for the actor. Once you increase the problems the obstacle causes, you help the actor find different tactics to solve his problem and thus increase the variety. Understanding the function of the obstacle is your secret weapon. Sometimes you pep up the obstacle by fiddling with the back story. "Another reason you don't want to move into that house is that his father has been flirting with you." It's more interesting to watch a woman scale a ten-foot wall than a three-foot wall. Plus the tougher the obstacle the deeper the concentration and the deeper the concentration the more compelling the action.

PICKING ON AN ACTOR

Actors, over a beer, will name names: The directors who are known in the profession to choose a whipping boy on each production. Actors will seldom confront a director on this cowardly habit because they can't afford to lose a job, but damage is done to the director's reputation in the profession and the director loses work. I take this practice to be a way of letting off steam for directors under pressure but it is nonetheless despicable. In life we find ourselves suffering a reverse chemistry that makes it difficult to stay in the room with certain people though we have no objective reason. When an actor's personality grates on you, be even more courteous and continue to direct them in the same way as the rest of the cast. Grace under pressure. Such situations can be supremely difficult, but the cast notices your restraint and your stature grows.

HANDLING THE
EMOTIONAL CRISIS

An actor becomes incredibly angry at you, throws her script across the room, and begins cursing. An actor, frustrated by the role and outside events, collapses to the floor and begins weeping. Don't mistake me, this won't happen often, but in a career of any length it's going to happen. As the circumstances will vary, all I can give is general advice. First, clear the room as quickly as possible so you can go one on one with the problem. Second, after letting the actor vent, ask the actor (or make you own judgment) whether she can continue. In either case make an appointment to see the actor before rehearsal the next day, which allows a cooling down period. If you need to rearrange the day's rehearsal, call the stage manager in and do so. Don't let the event shut down the work. Preferably do not discuss the problem with the cast when rehearsal resumes. Say Diana (or whoever) needs a break and will be back tomorrow. Most important, demonstrate that the work has the tensile strength to go on.

RULES OF REHEARSAL

They are theater traditions that have evolved out of the necessity of creating a good (and practical) working atmosphere. Some people know them, some people don't. It's your job to keep them in play without seeming like a martinet.

1. When people are late, they apologize to the stage manager, the director, and, in extreme cases, the room.

2. People leaving a scene or needing to get to the other side try not to walk in front of where the director is working.

3. Actors should know their lines on the date assigned.

4. People not in the scene should not read for pleasure or do taxes in the room. It implies the action is boring.

5. Any offstage conversation should be whispered and short. Also don't run lines out loud.

6. Actors may not leave the general area without checking first with the stage manager.

7. No smoking, no cell phones, no elaborate meals.

8. Don't direct on the breaks without asking permission. ("May I give you a note?")

9. Be presentable, wash hair, wash you.

10. Introduce visitors.

THE DIRECTOR AS HOST

In the best sense, the rehearsal is your party. It happens to be a creative party, a working party, but a party nevertheless. As host for this soirée, there are matters of manners and taste that fall under your aegis.

1. Know everyone's name.

2. Greet and say good-bye to each person.

3. Create an atmosphere of mutual respect.

4. Affirm good work.

5. Apologize when you are late.

6. Start on time, end on time, give breaks on time.

7. Never knowingly embarrass the participants.

8. Make sure that older actors are physically comfortable during the work.

9. Show the crucial courtesy of being prepared.

10. Gently assist others in understanding the courtesies necessary to the room.

And bring cookies to share!

MOMENTS OF REPETITION

A man waves good-bye to his daughter and then boards a train never to return. Several times during the production his dream figure repeats the gesture at key moments in her mind's eye. Repetition. The work of the great American director Anne Bogart makes startling use of this idea in both blocking and gesture. It has long been a staple of the cinema. In the main, we're in the world of symbol and metaphor and memory here. A gesture of submission is repeated several times by different characters during the course of a play in which it is a significant theme. Sometime repetition serves both beauty and sense — I recall André Serban's *Cherry Orchard* where Ranevskaya's profound feelings drove her to run in repeated circles until the viewer's heart almost burst. It can provoke understanding and unlock emotion when the repetition unlocks or drives home the center of the play. It can burn an idea into the mind of the viewer forever, or set up a joke they'll still be laughing at on the way home. Does it have a role in the work you're currently doing? Dip your toe in the water, experiment.

ON THE MONEY

This can be a compliment or a criticism. Used to affirm, it means that the actor or scene or act or play just functioned exactly as you wanted it. As a criticism it means the chosen solution is too obvious, too clear, unsurprising, and baldly put. The director always needs to sense what, if anything, must be added to the work the text does. If the textual moment is clear, the director mustn't push the actor to further demonstrate it. If the line is, "I love you," you obviously don't need to tell the actor to put his hand on his heart. If the line is, "Leave this house forever," must you tell him to point? The actor's and director's effort is to get under the line rather than to underline the obvious. You will find that "too much on the money" can happen with the set, the costumes, the sound score, the lights, the blocking, and the character's emotional life. It can trivialize the way the lines are spoken or the way a relationship is regarded. This is the virtue of clarity made ridiculous by overstatement. You'll find it in yourself as often as you'll find it in your cocreators.

THE EXTRA PAIR OF EYES

It doesn't matter how good you are, how experienced you are, how much you hate criticism; with a week to go you need a theater-smart empathetic friend or mentor to take a look at your work. Many directors never do this because they are afraid of what they may hear. Big mistake. You are getting too close to the work, you're beginning not to see the forest for the trees. At this point you may be working on a tiny detail and overlooking a central problem. Things you want to know at this point include: Is the story clear? Can you understand everyone and, if not, *where?* Is it obvious whose story the play is telling? Is there a section or scene that's just plain old boring? (Sorry, there probably is.) Is someone breaking the style? Is there a performance that's adversely affecting the play? Are there times when the actors aren't relating and responding? Are there things we're doing that are distracting and unnecessary? Once this pair of eyes has come, given notes, and gone, you need to sit in a quiet place and think which of these insights you buy and which you don't and what to do about the reactions you feel have merit. It's dangerous to go an entire rehearsal period alone. Bring in the eyes.

SCHEDULING TIME
IN REHEARSAL

A good and timely schedule is a theatrical virtue. It helps the entire staff and company. If possible you should give the stage manager your rehearsal schedule for three days at a time. If your style or other complexities make that difficult for you, give the stage manager tomorrow's schedule before you leave today's rehearsal. The schedule should list the scenes to be worked (page what to page what), the actors involved, and the time that scene will be called. As in:

12–12:45: Review blocking pp. 27–34.
  James, Washburn, and Helene.
12:45–1:30: Fight choreography pp. 41–43.
  Full cast.

and so on.

During the first two or three days of rehearsal, I'll cut myself some slack in case I run overtime, and I warn the actors it may happen. If I see a scene running long, I'll tell the waiting actors. You'll need to learn your own rehearsal rhythms to do accurate scheduling. It builds confidence, however, yours and the company's.

WHAT TO DO WITH WHAT
THE PLAY'S ABOUT

You've done your homework. You know what the play's about and can say it simply and clearly. Look at the play's major scenes and major speeches — how will they reflect and deliver the meaning? Itemize the major events of the narrative and examine how they are tied to this engine of the play. Continually take this sense of the meaning and tie it to specifics of the text. What are the exact lines that help the central characters reveal the theme? How can the actor and design team assist you? Often the playwright frames the central ideas in the negative: If the play tells us that only forgiveness allows the fulfilled life, then the bad things that happen to the character who can't forgive are also illustrations of the theme. The director uses the theme and its connections to the text to assist the actor in making choices and identifying crucial moments. Remember, this larger sense of the play *always* leads us to specific acting and directing moments *in the text*. This is not an intellectual exercise — it is a framework that allows each small choice to assist in revealing the play.

BEYOND PREPARATION

Beyond a certain point no set of ideas, no amount of preparation, guarantees the work. The sudden illumination, the intuitive breakthrough, the happy accident, and plain dumb luck play important roles. A single inspiration, a sudden instinct acted upon by the performer, can change the direction of a characterization. It doesn't happen often but suddenly, beyond any of our controls, everything can change. Preparation is not performance, it only attempts to create the conditions from which performance emerges. Directing is being enough in the moment to catch the tiny illuminations, instincts, and signs that are all around us in the artists we work with, waiting to be expanded. You never go into rehearsal only to pursue the ideas you have but open and eager to embrace the ideas that come. The preparation allows you to pay attention.

NOT TALKING

When is silence golden for the director?

1. When one of the actors is saying exactly what you would have said if you were talking.

2. When an actor's eyes glaze over.

3. When the actors are discussing a point among themselves in a helpful way.

4. When you truly don't know (say so).

5. When you've already interrupted a scene several times and they need to get some momentum going.

6. When an actor asks to try something.

7. When the actor needs a moment to think about something you've said.

8. When the actor is not doing what you wanted and he knows it.

9. When the room spiritually needs quiet.

10. When you've been doing a lot of talking already.

CREATING ATMOSPHERE

In Chekhov's *Seagull,* the author Trigorin speaks of creating a moonlit night for the readers by writing of the reflection off a shard of broken bottle. Once you are aware of the atmosphere you want, remember, like Trigorin, to do it with the details. Yes, of course you have sound and light at your disposal, but you also have rhythm, the emotions evoked in the actor, objects and their uses, and behaviors. How can an actor using a single object create a busy high school gym, a funeral viewing, a foggy night on the Golden Gate Bridge, an opening night party after a catastrophic review? What goes on between these characters to make what we call atmosphere?

I recently saw a scene where the echoing sound of the actor's footsteps paired with fluorescent light evoked the loneliness and menace of an empty, late night subway station. The text itself will create atmospheres that you can heighten with well-chosen detail. Here is a case where you need to increase your awareness of daily life. What is the atmosphere now? What makes it so? You need to read through your script thinking of the atmospheres and their uses. "Now, what can I do that evokes that?"

THE BEST IDEA IN THE ROOM

As a young director with an insecure ego I almost insisted that every idea in the rehearsal process be mine. I found it particularly hard to be gracious when an actor's suggestion proved to work better than mine. Looking back, I see how my need to be the only creative force made me ridiculous. Remember one thing: A good production is always thought to be a directorial success. The ideal rehearsal situation is one where the best idea in the room is adopted. For this to occur the director needs to make it clear early that she is open to suggestion. I often do it by admitting that a certain moment is unclear or confusing to me and openly asking for help. When good help is forthcoming, I try to celebrate it as well as adopt it. The real deal is that the actors don't expect you to know everything and become suspicious and alienated if you pretend you do. You are going to need all the minds available to do the best work. Actors will often lie back, not wanting to offend. Give the signal that you're eager for the good idea.

WHAT'S THEATRICAL?

Theatrical moments and conceptions are beautiful, shocking, surprising, and reveal the meaning of the play all at once. These theatrical devices can be visual, aural, rhythmic, violent, still, a single gesture, or an object at a key moment. What's going to be theatrical about this production — your production? You say the sofa will also be a coffin, a Man-of-War, a movie theater, and a bed? Grand. You say there will only be one chair and no one will sit in it until the final moment? Riveting. You say everything will be in slow-motion rhythm until she regains her sight? Excellent. You say the moment before she quits will be preceded by a thirty-second pause? Can't wait.

Every theatrical moment has a logic that reveals the play. But think theatrically. What's theatrical about the set, the lights, the sound, the costumes, the scene, the beat? Yet, don't put too many jellies in the fruitcake. Let us build our anticipation. Let us coast in neutral and then jam the accelerator to the floor. Rarity also defines the theatrical moment. Learn to think constantly of the *theatrical*, and how it might assist in the telling of the tale.

SAFETY

You, the *director,* are responsible for the safety of the actors. Often an actor will bend over, another actor leans over her. When the first actor straightens, her head hits the actor leaning over in the jaw, dislocating it. Whose fault? Yours. You have to be aware at all times of what's happening onstage and what may be dangerous. People climbing a ladder for the first time? You foot it. Someone on a second level too close to an edge without a railing? Stop the rehearsal. A dagger or kitchen knife dropped on the floor during a crowd scene? Stop the rehearsal. Someone slips and falls and then jumps to her feet saying everything is all right? Take five to be sure. It's your job to see the stairway unit that isn't locked down, the bottle too near the edge of the table, the broken leg on the sofa. Don't assume the stage manager should see these things and get you off the hook. When anyone gets hurt, it's your fault. Simple as that.

GETTING YOUR HEAD
IN THE ROOM

Directing is a concentrated endeavor. You need to be in the present moment with a careful schedule for the day and at least a few immediate goals. The first half hour of rehearsal is often wasted because the director doesn't have clear enough objectives, is still dealing with life outside the room, and is suffering self-consciousness due to lack of readiness. It's best to prepare for rehearsal as an athlete prepares for a game. You need sufficient rest, healthy food, a game plan, and some moments of inner quiet or meditation before you begin. If you are in rehearsal and feel your attention wandering, change your physical position, shake yourself gently, change what you're looking for, even move to a different part of the scene. When you catch yourself floating, move onto the stage and do a little close work on a four- or five-line sequence. Develop a personal alarm system for failing concentration.

ABOUT?

1. What's this play about?

2. What's this scene about?

3. What's that line about?

4. What's this moment about?

5. What's that move about?

6. What's this silence about?

7. What does he think her reaction is about?

8. What's this transition about?

9. What's their conflict about?

10. What's their relationship about?

11. What's this long speech about?

The word *about* is the director's dear friend. It equates to finding the meaning of whatever she's working on at the moment. The answer to "about" frames the acting decisions to be made. It makes choices possible and making choices within the circumstances is the director's work. If the actor asks, "What does this 'about' mean?" You can say, "Precisely, it's about the meaning." This word drives us further into the text, deeper into the moment. About opens the story like a flower.

WORKING LOOSE, WORKING TIGHT

The good director works in both these styles. Working loose is basically stimulating the actor by emphasizing the given circumstances and encouraging actors to make choices within them. While working loose the director may remind the actor of plot points, talk about larger actions for the scene, restate the obstacle, talk about the play's theme and the actor's character, and encourage the performer to "find" the blocking. Working tight is working and polishing very small units of text. Finding the action for a line instead of a beat. Making sure blocking punctuates the text. Looking on action and reaction in a four-line sequence. Polishing an entrance or exit or curtain line. Pulling an actor down on two or three lines that go over the top. Working the subtext in a single speech. The natural sequence of the director's process is from larger to small over the course of the rehearsal. I notice some directors are nervous about working tight. Don't be. Done well the actor appreciates it.

VARIETY

Work for it in all its incarnations.

1. Rhythmic variety in the speech and in the role. We're supposed to be playing some jazz here.

2. Spatial variety. Different relationships to the space and the architecture. Movement of different speeds.

3. Variety in the pace. Quick, slow, and in-between.

4. Variety of mood and atmosphere.

5. Emotional variety in the work of each actor and in the play as a whole.

6. Variety in the actor's personal tonality. Every actor has a particular musical speaking range. Make sure it isn't monotonous.

7. Variety inside the relationships. Every relationship needs variety in its exchanges and in the way it is experienced.

You're the maestro; make sure your orchestra explores all its possibilities.

SMALL PARTS

In the good production the small parts are well played, which implies significant attention from the director. The point is that you've got to meet with those actors, give them notes, and direct them in the scenes. Surprisingly, many directors don't. The director must discern the *function* of the small role, what it's there to accomplish in the larger narrative. Is the joke the taxi driver tells there to distract our hero so he forgets his wallet and is marooned in Dayton where he is mistaken for the president? Fine. It leads us to the style and energy the joke teller needs to make the role function. It also helps us understand what is too much, or not enough, in the playing. The director who treats the actor playing the small role with dignity and seriousness reaps the values of wonderful morale, cohesive ensemble, and probably a good reputation that will produce more work. In the play you're doing, is everyone getting at least a few minutes of your complete attention?

FAKING THE EMOTION

Because it is so hard for the director to approach emotion in the actor, and because we can only create the conditions, the surround in which the emotion might appear, we are at the mercy of the actor who is not emotionally available and connected. What do we do when the actor can do nothing but fake it? Oh my. Well, the hard truth is that this happens a lot. A few actors are so in tune with their feelings that their belief in the circumstances of the play allow an unforced, unmanipulated, and real flow of emotion perfect for the situation. All too often we must turn the actor upstage, allow him to cover his face, and resort to toning the faked emotion way, way down. Sometimes you can use repression as a tool and avoid embarrassing demonstrations of emotion that has become technique and nothing more. You can also cut down the length of the display or try to focus attention on the others who are reacting to the display. Mainly, have them do less.

Rehearsal
Process

THE DIRECTOR'S BRIEFCASE

1. Two copies of the script labeled with name, address, phone number. Have nontear binding and hole rings or you'll lose pages.

2. Sharpened pencils and a dozen of your favorite pens.

3. A penlight.

4. A clipboard.

5. Phone numbers for everyone on the production. (Don't wait till the second week!)

6. Plastic colored marker tabs for the scripts.

7. A pocket dictionary. Are you sure you understand the script's vocabulary? What's the difference between *irate* and *furious?*

8. Two letter-size yellow pads.

9. White-out.

10. A turned-off cell phone. (Don't get me started about cell phones in rehearsal.)

11. A copy of the rehearsal schedule. A copy of the production schedule.

12. Colored underliners and pens.

13. A list of things you want to do today. Included should be moments with the actors, not just scene numbers.

THE ACTIVE VOCABULARY

The great director Bill Ball said we need to use verbs, active verbs. Well, I don't care what the parts of speech are as long as our end of the conversation provokes a passionate desire to *do*. You need to describe the actors' opportunities and responsibilities in ways that make them itch to play the situation. The director's vocabulary must motivate, seduce, involve, intensify, and fascinate. The director is a spellbinder and pitchwoman for the power of the situation and circumstances. When you finish describing the fix the character is in and the high stakes that ride on the character's actions, the actor should be hot and steaming. Remember you are setting the bar and issuing the challenge. Some directors, once they know the play, do this as a matter of course. Others of us need to sit home and decide how we can describe the three-scene part as the role of a lifetime. Actors feed off the informed enthusiasm of the director. You need to make whatever preparation necessary to concentrate the actors' will and unleash their creativity. Like the volleyball coach who sends the team diving for balls outside their reach, you must inspire maximum effort.

THE ACTION IN ACTION

Usually the action is what we want the other person to do, feel or understand. When relationship is not the point it may simply be what the character wants. What are the action's uses to the director? Obviously to concentrate the moment or the scene on intent and to focus the actor's energy. The action provokes response and creates interplay. It functions as an antidote to generalization and grounds the actor who is for the moment at sea. It gets the actor and director on the same page where they can both work to clarify meaning. It promotes active inquiry but does not assume the director knows the answers. Used well it increases the stakes and heightens audience interest. Do you try to nail down the action for every beat? Of course not. You'd have to rehearse for a year. Ask the question when you feel the actors or the scene is drifting. If the actor doesn't know, you may have to hazard a guess. You may have to experiment with more than one action to get the scene on track. What seems perfect to you may not work for the actor. As a rule of thumb I probably ask about the action a half-dozen times in a five-hour rehearsal.

GESTURE

What is it? Where, in the actor, does it come from? Gesture is often the mysterious signing that emerges from the emotional storm. In its commonplace form, it describes, as in "I want one this big." Sometimes it's the outward marking of the rhythm of the speech, a kind of emotionally driven conducting. Sometimes it's potent because of its absence, because stillness has replaced it. Sometimes it's descriptive of character and how that body, and that body alone, works. It signifies by its strength, its weakness, its size.

Sometime, you may have to have a frank conversation about gesture with an actor. No, it's not a forbidden subject. Gesture is one of the subjects it's hard to talk around and achieve results. Say what's bothering you. Sit back at one rehearsal and concentrate on how gesture is assisting or hindering each performance. Is it defining character, releasing emotion, or simply distracting from the text? Is her body in her performance? You'll see something you want to work with or on.

BEATS AND THE DIRECTOR

I know, I know, in the past you've done the beats (which took hours) and then . . . never looked at them again. Why bother? Here's why. The beats create rhythm. The space between the beats is where the transition lies, and transitions are a basis of the actor's inner life. The end of a beat and the beginning of another is often where a blocking move begins or ends. In a comedy when you are overpaced, the end of a beat is a way to put the brakes on. With beats you can assist, and even enforce, the actor's thought process by requesting he makes clear how he got from point A to point B. Most important, the beat is a way of dividing up the play into actions, obstacles, and tactics (each beat has them). They also become part of your working rehearsal schedule. "I want to work the three beats starting with her entrance and going until he's electrocuted by the Hi-Fi." You'll be providing crucial variety by stopping actors from playing the same action over and over by reminding that when the beat changes, the action changes. The beats are a tool of definition and clarity. You'll need them.

TEN MISTAKES

1. Overpacing. Pace is the delivery system for meaning, not an end in itself. We need fast parts and slow parts even within a single speech.

2. Not blocked soon enough. The actor wants at least ten days before tech is completely blocked and book or script is gone to explore the role.

3. Overtalking. Talk is crucial. When it becomes repetitive or not directly related to the text, you're wasting precious time.

4. Assuming the actors want to block the play themselves (or can). They want you to make a shape and then let them try things inside it.

5. Paying no attention to rhythm. The actor can't control rhythm. The director must.

6. Creating a depressive, cold, humorless, over-critical atmosphere. Go figure!

7. Run-through after run-through. They know you don't know what to do now.

8. Picking on actors. They know you're insecure.

9. Letting the tech spin out of control. You're hopeless.

10. Not understanding the values of affirmation in the process.

TWELVE MORE MISTAKES

1. Your work shows you don't know what kind of play it is.

2. You're late a lot.

3. Outside the rehearsals you badmouth actors or the play.

4. You can't recognize a good idea unless it is yours!

5. You have no idea where the jokes are.

6. You get a reputation for treating staff people and technicians badly.

7. You work on some scenes too much and other scenes too little.

8. You treat creative artists as if they were children.

9. You don't collaborate.

10. You haven't used the time well and the play isn't really ready to open.

And let's not forget:

11. You spend a lot of crucial rehearsal time doing endless warmups.

12. People can't understand what the hell you're talking about.

THE GOD OF VARIETY

Let's take a wild stab and say that over fifty percent of what a director does and says has variety as its goal. When the audience is on to what you're doing, they want you to do something else. We seek variety in pace, characterization, emotions, mood, tone, response, action, obstacle, tactics, relationship. You name it, we want it to be varied. Often a single emotion persists beyond its welcome, or too much yelling or laughing, or the actor's voice lodges on one musical note and stays there.

The hard part is that when the director concentrates on making sure the rhythms are varied, he may overlook the actor's hand endlessly chopping the air. I often write on my hand (honest!) two or three categories I want to make sure have variety before rehearsal so I remember to look and listen for them. The God of Variety is merciless because when the actor doesn't have variety, or the scene doesn't or the way something is being done doesn't, the play dies a million deaths. Remember, the Pony Express rider never rode a horse until it died under him, and neither should you.

BUSINESS

The old character man looks wearily at the young director who is off on a philosophical rampage about something or other and sighs. "All I need is some business, dear, just a little something to do to show I'm on to him."

What's "business"? As soon as his son's wife leaves the room, he runs his finger under the edge of the table and inspects for dust. He then turns over a decorative porcelain figure to check the maker and holds up a supposedly crystal vase to the light. He hears her coming and sits down, a picture of innocence. He smiles as she enters. We know him before he speaks.

Whose idea was the business? A high percentage of the time it was the director. Business is the art of defining character or psychology or revealing plot through little things the actor does. Although we ordinarily don't want to be too "busy," we are forever on the lookout for the telling touch. Directors create business both on the spur of the moment in rehearsal and with malice aforethought at home at their desk. Look for these moments that say what the dialogue does not. It's visible text.

BACK STORY

Back story is what happened before the play or scene began. It's not described in the text. This is the only play stuff we "write." Good back story supports the basic circumstances of the text and gives background to the actor that allows true and more dramatic work within the writer's confines. Bad back story drives the actor in directions the rest of the text will not support. Who makes up the back story? Sometimes you do, sometimes the actor does, sometimes you do it together.

The director's job is to separate useful back story from its opposite. In a light comedy where a romantic relationship is foundering, we probably shouldn't posit that the problems are exacerbated because she was raped when she was a teenager. Rape isn't funny. That our heroine was once frightened by an IRS agent who looked like her boyfriend stays within the style. If it allows text to be played more richly it's good back story. If it throws the play off kilter, it's bad, bad back story. The director also uses back story to move the actors toward their goals.

PHYSICAL PUNCTUATION

Actors need to physically punctuate and heighten the words they are saying. Back in the pretraining days (yes, there were once actors who didn't have master's degrees!) the veterans kept saying to the neophytes, "Don't sit till the end of the line. Don't slam the door on a key word. Use the move to make the transition." These were the kinds of things people picked up by doing one-a-week stock, and everyone knew them.

Now, the director needs to know them and say them. Crossing on someone else's key line ruins focus, yes, but it also breaks the ancient rules of physical punctuation. So does wandering around. Gesture punctuates. Changing position punctuates. When you bite the sandwich punctuates. Expert directors break these rules with impunity because they know other tricks that render their apostasy harmless. As a painter learns the body before he abstracts it, practice physical punctuation before you disdain it.

WHEN YOU'VE LOST
YOUR TEMPER

Apologize. Calm yourself and apologize. Apologize to the whole cast if necessary. Apologize to the actor you hate and the stage manager who is driving you mad. Find a way to solve the problem other than showing off your mercurial moods. Temper tantrums are a misuse of your authority, and they usually bond the cast in opposition to you. Any good they do is usually short term, and the recipient of your tirade will either be turned on and eaten by the pack (which really doesn't help when you open on Thursday) or will find a way to pay you out, even if it takes years. You have dispensation to lose your temper once a decade. However you still have to apologize, even if it damn well wasn't your fault. Temper poisons the atmosphere and even the guiltless get frightened and cease (for a time) to do their best work. Trust me, it's not worth it.

THE ECOLOGY OF REHEARSAL

Rehearsal is an organism. The director must understand that each element and person involved in the rehearsal process affects all the others. The director must keep a weather eye on the health and function of the entire process. If one actor continues, say, to radiate negativity, it can destroy the rehearsal process for everyone. If, for instance, one actor is not giving to and affecting the others, it can be the beginning of creative starvation for all. The director must tend the room as well as the play. She must sense if there is a general lassitude or a sense of panic or general ill feeling and work to stabilize it. When the rehearsal's ecology is functioning well, the director can afford a low profile, but there are also times to step forward and minister to the atmosphere and the problems that are doing it harm. "How's the room?" the director reminds herself. "What are the room's needs?"

RARITY

I've mentioned this in other tips, but I want to emphasize its uses. Here's the director's equation: The later in the play you do something for the first time (we're talking blocking here), the more focus it has. You know, sitting in the one rocking chair, going over and touching the urn that holds your grandfather's ashes, opening the refrigerator in your lover's apartment. Rarity on stage gives value much the same way it does in the art market. You want to make use of this rarity in a way that *reveals* the text. You use the piece of blocking you've been saving for a key psychological or narrative moment. For heaven's sake don't save it only to waste it. This concept of rarity does not only apply to blocking but to gesture, to weeping, to the costume that tells us everything, to the special sound cue and an amazing look in lighting. Remember not to use your best opportunities in a profligate manner. Support the important moments that reveal the central theme with a look, a sound, a sit, or a rhythm you've been saving. It's meaning in the bank.

MINIMALISM

It can be sexy to do less. If there isn't a lot of movement, what there is can startle. Sometimes holding stillness longer than expected feels explosive. You take such risks when the text itself or the scene's tension is fascinating enough to beat the weight of stasis. When we wait for release, simplicity teases us and increases our concentration. Where, in the play you are currently working on, would doing less make a crucial scene or moment more interesting? Scenes before or after heavy moments are always good candidates. Remember that some conversations are so interesting, so dangerous, so loaded with possibilities that the addition of movement only vitiates. It's also true that more and then less and then more provides an attention-grabbing variety in tempo and use of space that can be extremely effective. Don't be seduced by the idea that if everything isn't in motion, it won't hold attention. Before you deem a scene ready to open check once more to see if a little weeding will sharpen the focus.

VISITORS IN REHEARSAL

Everybody has their own idea about visitors. Mine is that I like a demystified rehearsal process. I'm put off by the idea that making plays is a precious, secret, sacred process. Now, that said, some scenes, moments, run-throughs, and particular actor's psyches need privacy. The working team, designers, wardrobe people, firearms experts need to have sufficient access and feel welcome. Also I usually extend professional courtesy to other theater workers and the visits of lovers, lawyers, and parents from Hawaii. Large numbers every day? Nope. Occasionally? You bet. It can even add a little positive edge with everyone taking their game up a notch. Always, always introduce the visitor to the cast so they have no reason to fear them. Ask that people enter on the breaks and leave on the breaks. If someone walks in you don't know, it's the stage manager's job to inquire.

WHY IS IT BEAUTIFUL?

You've blocked the play. The actors are off book. Maybe you're even having a run-through. You're beset with details. You already see there isn't enough time. You hate the actor Jack and the designer Joan. The last thing you're worrying about is the aesthetics. Wrong. Worry. One of the greatest pleasures in the theater is sudden unexpected beauty. It could be the meld of set and costumes or the actors in space or the intricacy of a complex speech or deep and profound emotion in the context of the story. It could be a rhythm or a matter of color or an amazing effect or a single gesture. We need to think about it even in a realistic or behavioral script. What is the "beauty" we will be providing the audience? Beauty is always theatrical. Audiences remember it years later with gratitude and affection. Sometimes we're so busy that we forget to include it in our arsenal and thereby lose a key opportunity to make theater essential.

PACE

This tip could be book length. Let's just call pace the rate at which given material can be revealed, understood, and command the audience's attention. The skimpier the emotional, intellectual, and psychological content, the quicker it can be taken in and processed. My father's theatrical generation would say you never want the audience to get ahead of you. Indeed, it is helpful to make them work a bit to keep up, but excess speed also flattens out material so that everything sounds the same and seems to have the same importance.

The phrase "no fast without slow" assists. Rather than fast or slow, good work is made up of varying rhythms suited to the text's situations, emotions, and content. Acting detail and speed are often in conflict. We must remember that pace is a delivery system for meaning. Extremely rapid work often seems an actor's parlor trick where we are simply amazed by the actor's ability to do it. The moment dictates. How quickly dare we fill it? We need to get the point; on the other hand we don't want to wait around after we've got it. General pace notes are dangerous, sometimes downright destructive. It's best to work in small increments and keep variety as a goal. Make sure pace is a function of the text and not of your personal fears.

IMAGES

The director seeks indelible images that burn themselves into our minds and strike to the heart of the
play. To make these images you must first find the
play's center, its motive force, its fiery lesson, its
deepest human understanding. Now look for what
can communicate these things without words.
Among others, those images might be:

1. A use of space we've seldom seen.

2. A surprising use of color and form.

3. An activity that encapsulates character and play.

4. Emotion in harmony or conflict with the space
   around it.

5. A grouping as metaphor.

6. Something made or destroyed before our eyes.

7. An object and a person bound together that give
   us a new understanding.

8. Extraordinary use of objects, cloth, wind, water,
   or fire.

9. Silence or sound that bonds with image.

10. A gesture in space that means everything.

Or the one, more apt, that you find to reveal the play.

FOCUSING ON THE CHARACTER YOU'RE AFRAID OF

Directors (surprise, surprise) like and understand some characters better than others. Some major characters either bore them or seem in broad outline too obvious to endure. Less obvious, sexual bias in often a factor, with male directors focused on male characters and female directors the opposite. This is a problem both in preparation and in the rehearsal room. Some dark night in the quiet of your room go through the play from the perspective of the characters you know you're ignoring. Over and over I've noticed directors attending less to the more passive characters in the scene. The director tends to put her energy where the energy lies. This selective focus then dislocates the scene and usually results in work where the relationship between the passive and active characters seems not to exist or to have been abandoned. Beware. You need to keep a weather eye on your character preferences and develop a personal warning system that can make you aware of your mistake.

THE COSTUMES AND YOU:
THE REHEARSAL PERIOD

The show is now being built in the shop or shopped in the stores, or both. If it's a shopped show, the renderings are only approximations of what the designers hope to find. The colors and patterns available will dictate. If you are particularly interested in or worried about certain costumes, find out when you may see them on the rack or, more important, when you may be present at the fittings. If you don't take advantage of these opportunities in process, it's bad form to be horrified at the tech.

When you attend fittings remember the politics of the fitting room. You agreed on the renderings. Possibly you have said you liked these clothes on the rack. Now, when the actor is involved, respond carefully. The actress hates the dress and wants to wear something of her own. The experienced designer will handle the situation, but remember, you want the actress to be comfortable, but you don't want to interfere with the design. Say you and the designer are aware of her needs and will talk further. When alone with the designer ask if there is a compromise that can serve all parties. Usually a third way that serves both the design and the actor's concern will be found. Don't allow the actor to put the designer in an untenable position.

WATCHING REHEARSAL

It's greatly difficult to watch rehearsal creatively. Attention wanders. Concentration fails. Most difficult of all, we often lose the sense of what we might be watching for. Here's a list I made for myself.

1. Circumstances: Which are currently applicable?
2. Action: Are the actors pursuing a goal?
3. Obstacles: What's keeping them from getting what they want?
4. Clarity: Am I getting it? Words and plot.
5. Interplay: If he does this, would she do that?
6. Folding in: Does this moment illuminate some other moment in the play?
7. Blocking: Is there something better?
8. Theme: Does this tie in to the play's meaning?
9. Is this theatrical?
10. Character: How does this define it?
11. Words: Are they being used, selected, and enjoyed?
12. Relationship: What's going on between these people?
13. Creativity: Is something happening, or is this last week's work?
14. Beauty: Is there any? Could there be?
15. Repetition: Do we need to do this again?

OPPOSITES

This is a key directorial tool. Stanislavski speaks about this idea often. Whatever the actor is playing, whatever goes on in a relationship, whatever the character's manner and sense of herself, look for at least one moment where the direct opposite is played. In Juliet's balcony scene, a feast of idealistic young love, find one moment of cynicism. In Hedda Gabler's agony of boredom, find the scene where she is fully engaged, even excited. In *Richard III,* find the moment of sentiment. Because of its rarity, it will strike home with the audience, so make sure it does something useful for you. It's a repeated mistake for the actor to ride one horse until it dies under him. Opposites go a long way toward solving that problem. The director wants to achieve complexity without creating confusion about just who the character is. A couple of opposites can get that done.

OPENING MOMENTS/
FINAL MOMENTS

The infamous and skillful boxer Willy Pep fought
well into his forties (some say fifties) basing his strategy on a single, simple perception, "Nobody remembers nuthin' but the first fifteen seconds and the last
fifteen seconds of the round." Although it's not quite
that clear in our world, it's still practical information. Put extra work into the openings and closings
of acts and the last couple of minutes of the play. If
it's one of those twenty-scene deals that contemporary playwrights love, you still put in the extra time
on beginnings and endings. These bits of the play
need to be thoroughly examined and given sufficient
repetitions to shine. This work gives the actors extra
confidence as well. When actor nerves are part of
the equation, it's nice to be completely in charge of
the opening ten minutes of the play. By that time
actors are into the rhythm, warmed up, and on a roll.

WORKING THE EXPECTATIONS

The director often surprises and pleasures the viewer
by messing with the audience's expectations. People
think they will see gnarled witches in robes and
instead they see odd feral children. They assume,
from everything they know, that a character will be
furious and instead she is amused. They expect a
melancholy Dane, and you give them a passionate,
rough-hewn man of action. Think as you go into a
scene what the audience's expectations will be and
what surprises are possible that still operate within
the circumstances. In a sense you are always fight-
ing to make sure that the audience doesn't get ahead
of the play. Just when they think they have your
production figured out you plan a reversal. Once
you've pulled a couple of surprises the audience continually wonders what's next? A reversal operates
as a kind of directorial suspense syndrome and
increases the quality of attention. Remember, these
reversals of expectation still have to serve the play.

BAD UNS

Directing the antisocial character or even the antisocial act takes some thought. If the theft, abuse, murder, or manipulation is the act of a character for whom we are ultimately to have sympathy, we work on it one way. If it's a character we're allowed to abhor, another. In the first case, our ordinary use of the action applies (what you want the other person to do, to feel, or to understand). Thus the negative action occurs out of frustration within the relationship, a mistaken instinct on others' behalf, or on behalf of some ultimate end seen as good for both or all. With the through-and-through bad un, the other is taken out of the equation and the action is simply "what I want." This want can then be completely self-serving or even mad. "I live to see that look in someone's eye the moment before they die." Now, even the worst of stage humanity often benefit from some contrary characteristic. The blackheart who rapes and pillages but also brings his mother flowers. Oh, and there's another category, the over-the-top villain as in *Richard III* and Captain Hook, and these fascinating monsters must be cast with one additional crucial quality: charm.

LOUDER AND FASTER

Ah yes, the actor's satire of the director who knows nothing else. Historically, "louder and faster" is a desperate bid to catch and hold the audience's attention. On the other hand, let's not be too dismissive. At bottom, we're talking about stage energy here and it is a precious commodity. There are moments when louder is necessary, both for audibility and command. I've sometimes given a veteran actor a long psychological justification and had them smile wryly and say, "Oh, you mean louder." And I did. I now empower you to say louder when that's what you mean. It's one of the few pieces of direction that can be immediately understood. As to faster we are in more dangerous territory, but as we work a scene for meaning I may say, "Eventually the rhythm here will be quick." I'll work small sections for a quick tempo but build in rests so it doesn't go on too long. Louder and faster has pitfalls as a general note but value as a specific one. You can laugh when you say it.

UNSTICKING THE IDEA

Are you stuck with your first idea for the blocking, for the ground plan, for the nature of the relationship? Is the actor stuck with his first reading, the time he sits, the action, the super objective? Ideas are almost never the problem, there are more where our first one came from. The problem is being locked into one idea before you've tried others. Remember that things can be sketched, tried, and discarded. Time limits experiment, but we mustn't behave as if it had outlawed it. As your craft grows you'll be less worried about discarding (possibly for a day or an hour) your first idea. If you roughblock the play within the first third of your allotted rehearsal period, you have the second third to experiment and the last to polish a chosen form. Try a little something different each day with something that's been previously set. Unlock the actors on a couple of lines, change a cross, find something new between the lovers. Tell yourself that almost anything could be up for grabs if you chose it to be. The third idea might be the one.

THE MAJOR ARCS

Better start by revisiting the definition of an arc, huh? I mean it's a lot more interesting when the character is different at the end than they were at the beginning. Now, I know that Joe the doorman, with three lines in Act One and seven in Act Two, may not be a great candidate for an arc. The leading roles, however, are. The director needs to decide where the text wants them to end up, emotionally and logically, and the director doesn't want that change to appear in the first scene. As a matter of fact, work on the arc then allows you to work backwards. It's the same strategy as a fireworks display. You don't want the big finale to be a repetition of anything else. Whether the director defines the arc to the actor or encourages a difference is a matter of personal style or situation. One more thing, on this journey, what moments in the text are important stations along the line? Sometimes I schedule a rehearsal where Scene One and Scene Ten are played back to back; it'll tell you if there's a viable arc.

THE BUILD

The build is a series of lines (usually four to six) where neither party wants to allow the other to have the last word or end up on top. During the build, each of the lines gets louder, capped by the final line. It's a vocal war over a given subject. The build ends because one person gives in, fears going further, refuses to be drawn into the fight, is disgusted or worries it is going too far. The build is a minor explosion, dramatic or comedic, that catches the audience's attention and whets their appetite for things to come. Usually the build occurs in moments of conflict but sometimes it's simply high spirits or friendly competition. Writers write builds all the time and directors often miss them, losing a spicy dramatic moment. The director needs to go through the script and identify the builds, point them out to the actors, rehearse them, and give notes if they later disappear. Often, to put it simply, they end up being a loud moment in a quiet scene. There is usually a pause at the end of the build as the characters think over where the jousting has left them.

STAYING ON TIME

Okay, this is going to be a little uptight, obsessive, even . . . well . . . anal. Directors should work to stay on time. Everybody, and I mean *everybody* appreciates it! What am I talking about here? There are going to be meetings that include other busy people—be on time. Start your rehearsals on time. Take your breaks on time. You won't always be able to stick to the day's rehearsal schedule, but when you're not able to, it should bloody well be an exception. You should stop rehearsal on time. There are lives to lead as well as plays to make. You should be at fittings on time, and a double curse on you if you don't make production meetings on time. People on a production look to you to set the tone. If an extra ten minutes doesn't matter to you, why should it matter to them? You should be at rehearsal fifteen minutes before it begins in case someone needs a private chat with you. Always, always, always apologize when you are late. It's both good theater ethics and a theater tradition. See what I mean . . . anal.

EGOS ON PARADE

Don't:

1. Don't work to make yourself the visible center of the experience.

2. Don't keep talking beyond the point that actually relates to the work.

3. Don't make a display of your anger.

4. Don't make demeaning jokes about the actors' work.

5. Don't make a general show of your concerns in the tech.

6. Don't move around so much in rehearsal that you are a distraction.

7. Don't treat the rehearsal as if you were a stand-up comic.

8. Don't spend a lot of time in the dressing rooms.

9. Don't spend a lot of time onstage.

10. Don't use note sessions to punish.

Your ego isn't the work.

TOO SOON

Directors often worry about getting there too soon. The fear is that everything will go stale and the audience will be served without verve and spontaneity. In practice this usually means that the play has reached a sort of performance level, and the director is overusing runthroughs to pass the time because she has no idea how to further improve it. If you sense you're having that problem, you probably need to direct even more from the actor's point of view. Are the actors playing actions or have they regressed to playing the sound they think the scene should have? Check the arc for each major character. Does the blocking give pleasure to the viewers? Are you using the bottom ten percent of the stage? Is your production theatrical? How can you increase those values? Are the ends of the scenes and acts crisp? Which actors still need help? Are there parts of the stage you haven't used? Listen, does the play have a variety of spoken rhythms? The play gets there too soon when the director runs out of ideas.

PLAYING AT
PERFORMANCE LEVEL

Very often you're rehearsing with a much smaller volume of space than you'll be performing in. I can't tell you the number of times I've allowed the actors to play at a more intimate level in rehearsal only to lose the play in the transfer to the larger space. Sizing up is particularly dicey with the less experienced actor. They begin hearing their own voice when you move onstage, which makes them lose concentration and become self-conscious. The hard truth is that you must push the actors to play at performance level in the rehearsal hall so that they're used to the sound and find nuance amidst the noise. Press to get into the space early for everyone's sake. Even just to test a scene or two and let the realities inform the actor. It's particularly crucial in comedy where one uses different technique to get the laughs dependent on the size of the house. My father used to pat young actors on the shoulder and say, "You have to play beyond the walls," to address this very problem.

THE DIRECTOR'S KAMA SUTRA

1. Say "You don't have to do the kiss till you're ready."

2. Work to make people who have physical involvement in a play like each other.

3. Anything that could embarrass the actor should be done first alone in a room attended by only you and the stage manager.

4. Make sure the actors know about any intimacy demanded before they agree to do the role.

5. Any onstage sex should be choreographed down to the last sigh.

6. If nudity is demanded and agreed upon, it's best kept out of the process until you move onto the stage.

7. If there are revealing costumes, the designer should speak about it to the actor before the first rehearsal. The actor should see any such renderings before the rest of the cast sees them.

8. The director's attitude to all such matters in rehearsal should be dignified and professional. No prurience and no jokes.

WHO NEEDS THE HELP?

You're about to open, a couple of actors are wonderful, several are adequate, and then there's . . . Jack. Well, it's too late now, you should have helped him a week ago. You must, sometime toward the halfway mark in rehearsal, step back and identify the actors who are in trouble. When it turns out they aren't talented enough, you either have to replace them or hide them (keep them sitting, cut down the line load, give them props to play with, hundreds of ways). If it's a confidence problem, build it. If they work slowly give them more rehearsal time and repetitions. The key factor here is to recognize the problems while there is still time to work on it. Many directors suffer from avoidance in this area, plus as we all know, it's more fun to direct the best people doing the best work. Take the actor in trouble away from rehearsal and level about the problem. Be specific, what part of what scene sucks? Give them your best private tutorial and see them again after rehearsal the next day. Praise improvement and be dogged. Never give up and never avoid. And see it in time.

SHEER FUN

Don't let the logical and intellectual side of the director's work dim the illumination that high spirits can provide. I remember when sheer bravado led Delroy Lindo as Othello to eat the letter that recalled him to Venice. No logic could have provided the moment. In fact logic might have cut it before its emotional rightness was recognized. In an otherwise forgettable comedy I once saw an actor pressed to leave a restaurant, cram his meal into his pockets as he flew out the door. I can't imagine the moment was prepared in anyone's study. The director creates the supportive atmosphere and underlying structure where intuitive madness feels welcome. I love the moments when we are laughing and saying, "No, no try that, go ahead do it, do it now!" Lunacy and logic make a great theatrical marriage. Don't bludgeon one with the other. They need each other.

REBLOCKING

Why is it that when we've blocked it, we think it's done? Why is it so hard to go back? Partially it's an admission we don't want to make and partially it's because we're pressed for time. When it's bothering you, bite the bullet and redo it. Usually the actors have been thinking the same thing and are relieved. Seriously. Why would our first idea be the best idea? Sometimes a seemingly boring or flaccid scene is amazingly revitalized by new architecture. Actors always like it when such work is prefaced by a brief explanation of why and what's being aimed for. They will seldom resist if the explanation is persuasive. There is, of course, a time toward the end of the rehearsal period when such renovations jangle nerves. Try not to do it in the last three days before tech unless you know the actors well and they are skilled. Reblocking is usually preceded by a clear idea about same but time permitting, it can also be experimentation as long as other important work isn't neglected. It isn't mandated that you have to live with your mistakes.

BITS AND PIECES

When I was a young actor, a director I worked for a great deal used to relish what he'd call the "bits and pieces period." This would occur in the four or five days before tech. There would be a run-through in the late afternoon, but before that he would schedule about three hours work in five- to fifteen-minute increments. He'd work on six lines here where he didn't like the rhythm, an entrance there, the beginning and ending of scenes, a busy physical moment, a fight, a section that had to be timed for someone's offstage change, a moment when an actor needed to push the energy, all manner of things that could be solved with short intensive work. It was exhilarating and confidence-building because one thing after another got better and you felt you were on a roll. Which, I might add, was part of his strategy. Adopting his methodology I often save little things I could have solved earlier for this period. It makes the actors feel ready for anything.

REPLACING THE ACTOR

The worst thing you'll ever have to do. You cast them, they can't do it, there's no point in trying again, the moment has come. First there is a point of no return, and you must recognize that and act in a timely manner. You do more harm by avoiding the decision than you do by implementing it. This is a private matter, and it should take place well away from rehearsal. When you sit down with the actor, don't let the event overextend. This is a subjective decision on your part; you don't feel the work is serving the play. Having said that, you've said everything. What follows is likely to be recrimination or unseemly pleading. Don't argue or debate. Don't be defensive or mean-spirited. Be clear, give what comfort you can, and move on to the details of the change. The actor should not return to rehearsal. Be businesslike *and* kind.

RUN-THROUGHS

How many? Maybe four before tech. Fewer and the
actors haven't had sufficient chance to absorb the
shape of the play. More and they may lose their edge
or become too technical. Of course it varies with the
demands and complexities of each text. During run-
throughs the director notes sections that need more
work, and checks the arcs of the major roles to make
sure the characters develop. He notices if there is sufficient variety in the blocking, pace, tone, and indi-
vidual acting. He watches how the focus is handled.
Are we looking where we need to be looking? Is the
story being told? Are some sections too busy and/or
the actors are working too hard? Is the energy delivering the play? Are there places where we need to
pull back? Run-throughs are usually followed by
working rehearsals that address your notes. A sure
sign that the director is losing touch with the work
is a schedule of run-through after run-through without rehearsals to address the problems made visible.

LEAVING REHEARSAL

1. The director should thank everyone in the rehearsal room for the day's work.

2. The director should not rush off. Stay a few minutes in case someone needs you.

3. Make sure you have a copy of tomorrow's rehearsal schedule.

4. Have an obligatory five-minute meeting with the stage manager.

5. Check twice to see that you have your script. It's embarrassing to have an actor hand it to you the next day.

6. Before you go back to the hurly-burly of your life, find a quiet corner and reflect on the day's work. If you wait till later you won't remember the crucial details. What problems will you need to address? What did the rehearsal clarify for you? Think back on the actor's work. Who did what badly or well? Make a few notes on sections you'll want to work in the next few days.

7. Close the door and have a life for a few hours. All work and no play. . . .

WORKING TOWARD THE END

Take in the end. Understand the end. Work toward the end. The playwright can't help it, she has an innate need for summation. If it's a plot-driven play, the event we've been preparing for occurs in the last ten pages. If it's character-driven it's those same pages that deliver the enlightenment or destruction (often self-destruction) that completes the role. Read the last pages over and over. Then trace backward the threads that got us there. You need to assist the actors in the process of becoming what's necessary at the end. What foreshadowing is there in the characters? Looking back what gesture should we have noted, or piece of business or line that later shows us the end in the beginning? *Hedda Gabbler* is, in a sense, one long struggle against the gunshot she finally cannot resist. Directing is the process of building the bridge that the play at last crosses. We don't simply work moment to moment, we prepare, we make ready. By understanding the end we can plot our course. The director needs to earn the ending.

Comedy

COMIC BUSINESS

Careful, it often isn't funny. A good piece of business proceeds from and further reveals situation and character. An actor getting tangled up in a phone cord as he talks either needs to increase his frustration at an inopportune moment, reveal the character's ineptitude, fear of objects, and impracticality or set up a subsequent moment when his boss walks in. The business is usually not funny in and of itself. In most cases the situation should not stop for the comic business. The business is propelled by the situation and, in turn, propels the situation. The other crucial element is the character's attitude toward the business. Slipping on a banana peel isn't in itself amusing, it's our sense of *that* character slipping and her response during and after that makes the comic moment. Often the best business is invented not by you but by the actor. But whomsoever is its creator, carefully measure the business by your developed sense of "too much." The style of the play guides you here. Does anything else written in the play support such a flight of fancy?

DIRECTING COMEDY

I had a director who in rehearsal sounded an electric buzzer after what he assumed were laugh lines. Don't do that.

1. Emphasize situation.

2. Help the actors passionately believe in the absurd circumstances.

3. Don't overload the play with funny business unless it's built in.

4. Work on the set-ups for the jokes.

5. The quote is, "Dying is easy, comedy is hard." Don't underestimate the work these plays take.

6. Don't imagine you can teach comedy to humorless souls.

7. Don't move on without giving sufficient repetition.

8. Don't (really don't!) get caught playing for laughs that aren't there.

9. The best comic directors are capable of "showing" the moment to the actor. Are you?

10. Exaggerated truth. Work for it.

11. Repeat and polish. It must look confident.

COMIC VARIATIONS

1. Low comedy: Don't attempt if you have no talent for knockabout or if you don't have skilled physical comics. A dangerous form.

2. Character comedy: What it says. Emphasize character and conflict generated out of character. Direct with the usual tools, straightforward with a light touch. No gimmicks.

3. High comedy: Rich people having fun. A sort of straightforward work but must, must, must know (or research) the manners and mores of the group, country, and period. Actors need charm and must wear clothes well. Impossible to do with the under twenty-five set.

4. Farce: the information delivered is simple so you can use a quick tempo. Takes more rehearsal time because of elaborate blocking and business. Best results with experienced actors. Clarify plot.

5. Romantic comedy: Needs attractive actors with a subtle sense of humor. God help you if they don't have chemistry. More in the line of character comedy. Highly detail the relationship.

Be very, very careful with casting in all these forms. Don't go for jokes that aren't in the writing. Deliver charm.

THE COMEDY LIST

1. Something funny is more likely to be out of proportion than in proportion.

2. Comedy demands delight in the playing.

3. Comedy is serious exaggeration.

4. Comedy uses surprise. Don't let the audience get ahead of the joke.

5. Comedy comes from overemphasis and under-emphasis and knowing when to use which.

6. The comic actor has profound belief, and concentration, while pursuing eccentric goals.

7. The joke and the reaction together form the laugh.

8. Comedy demands the confidence of the actor. It is, in a sense, a lion tamer's gig.

9. Timing is the art of the pause (or the lack thereof) before the set-up and before the joke. Watch the experts and experiment.

10. Don't so overpace comedy that there is no place for the audience to get in and laugh.

MORE COMEDY

1. Get the comedy into the body as well as the text.

2. Make sure the set-up is heard.

3. Make sure the joke is heard and in the clear.

4. Make sure the reaction to the joke is seen.

5. The better the joke the less you have to push it.

6. If the set-up comes in high, undercut it. If it comes in low, top it.

7. The best comic writers set it up so the character does the right thing at the wrong time or the wrong thing at the right time. Look for it.

8. Changing the tempo of the scene at the moment of the joke may help the laugh.

9. You can sometimes increase and lengthen the laugh by keeping the reactions coming after the laugh starts.

10. The last week of rehearsal without an audience can convince you it was never funny and drive you to excess. Hang in there, they'll laugh.

COMIC TONE

Is is possible to nail down how the actor plays differently in a comedy than in a drama? Well, not quite but almost. Comedy demands an energy in the playing that is by its very nature life-affirming. Let's put it this way, depression in comedy is energetic. In comedy, the small things are played as if they were big things. In tragedy, Lear is distraught by the loss of a kingdom. In comedy, Joey is distraught because he forgot to bring home asparagus. The sound of an argument in a drama is dark and dangerous. The sound in comedy is appalled, annoyed, thunderstruck, but we always get the sense from the sound that whatever it is, it's survivable. There is an "I can't believe this is happening, wake me up," sound to catastrophe in comedy. You never believe from the sound that anyone will be hurt or that suicide is possible. No one in comedy is ever a victim of child abuse. The more negative the moment, the more absurd the character's reaction. Comedy is often ferocious, but just beneath the ferocity is the belief it can still turn out well. Listen.

THE RELEASE FOR THE LAUGH

All right, Bobby the actor moves from the French window (they don't do French window plays anymore) to above the sofa, delivers his side-splitting laugh line about the alligator in the bathtub, and then what? The laugh hits and rolls on for ten endless seconds. What does Bobby do then? Bobby releases. While the laugh continues, he moves over and sits beside Betty to whom he will direct his next line. The good comedy director blocks for the laugh. He makes sure the inner life of the characters and the narrative life of the play continues even though dialogue is on hold for the audience's reaction. Will you always know where the laugh will fall and how long it will continue? Of course not. On the other hand, lots of times you will. Give the actors something to *do* during the laugh. It's a perfect time to set the comic or emotional tone for the next moment. Readjust the picture. Get to a prop that's needed. The laugh, once it hits, gives the director a brief time to prepare the next beat. Use it.

The Final Stage

NOTES NEAR OPENING

By the time you reach the last few days before tech you should be building the confidence of the company. A good many of your notes should be affirmative, "I particularly liked. . . ." Even if you're far from sanguine about the outcome, building confidence is likely to get you further than communicating danger. By now you are working on smaller and smaller sections, and each rehearsal has a couple of hours of "bits and pieces." Your notes reflect the same progression from the general to the specific. You should be remarking on single moments now, single lines, single subtexts. Whatever you do, *don't* say things like, "Well, the whole thing has got to play faster," or "The scene needs to be angrier." The actor taking general notes at this point may erase weeks of careful work by emphasizing a single quality. Don't generalize now, it's dangerous.

POLISHING

The ideal rehearsal process unfolds so that you are ready to open three or four days before tech. No, it's not perfect, far from it, but if you had to show the work to an audience, you would not be embarrassed. They could pay for what you've got. In these remaining days there are run-throughs, yes, but you reserve at least a couple of hours for polishing. This means making moments shine, putting fifteen minutes into an eight-line section to raise the stakes, making the blocking concise, enforcing a build, giving an extra dollop of safety to a slap or punch, making sure the sound of a door slam doesn't obscure an important word or phrase. Your polishing schedule breaks down each rehearsal hour into four to eight segments (yes, sometimes you book as little as five minutes to work a single moment). During this time you pay extra attention to the beginning and ending of scenes, entrances, and exits, highly physical moments, a cross where an actor looks uncomfortable, touches of physical comedy, scene transitions, and elaborate work with props. This is often the difference between average and good. Make the time.

THREE MORE TIMES WHEN YOU CAN DO THAT

Toward the end of rehearsal when you and the actor have accomplished the major shaping of the role, it becomes clearer what *isn't* there and what you need more of. The best possible circumstance is to identify a moment the actor is already doing. Let's say the role is a horrible, scheming, dangerous, manipulative bad guy, but the actor plays this one moment of simple, sensitive kindness. Point to that moment and say, "Now you need to find three more times where you can do that." The advantage of approaching it this way is that it doesn't sound like an overwhelming task and it leaves (at least for the time being) the creative decision-making to the actor while clearly saying what is needed. What you're looking for is not a major characteristic of the role but a kind of seasoning that adds a different taste, a different color. Doing whatever it is three more times won't change the role but it will sophisticate it, make it more complex. Keep your eyes open, and then ask for more.

THE SPACING REHEARSAL

The first time I received a tech schedule with this phrase prominently displayed, I had no idea what it was. In many (but not all) theaters time is allotted at the beginning of tech, usually without lights, sound, or costumes, for the director and actors to move out of the rehearsal room and onto the stage to check whether the planned blocking works well on the set. Almost invariably you turn out to need the time. The scene you played on the stair landing has sight-line problems. The scene with the actors clustered around the dining room table now looks lumpy and claustrophobic. Space (the nice open space in the rehearsal room) always impacts composition differently when you add the walls. Usually you can make good use of five hours of spacing on the set. Inquire early of the powers-that-be if time will be devoted to spacing in the tech period. Request it. Fight for it. It's a good thing.

HANDLING TECHS

The tech needs to be organized, forward-moving, calm, positive, and a good problem-solving atmosphere. The director deflects any sign of panic or confrontation, is concerned for safety, empathetic with the actor, has goals for the time, and is respectful of all the departments' processes. The dour, grim, angry director slumped and isolated, paranoid and unpredictably explosive is the nightmare version. Don't jump all over the designer's rhythms (particularly lights and sound). Gently ask what's causing a long holdup. Give the actors breaks. Don't keep actors long in heavy costumes. Try not to call needless attention to yourself in an officious or show-offy style. If you can solve a problem, do so. If others are solving it, don't interfere. Don't undercut the stage manager's authority. This should basically be their tech to run. Before the tech, set goals with the designers and technicians. After the tech, gather for mutual notes. Check in with each actor to see how he or she is doing. If some area's work is slow or late, make sure you find out why and try to avoid public protest. Still direct when you can. Troubleshoot where it's valuable. Be firm when useful but always human.

THE CURTAIN CALL

What's it there for? It exists so that the audience may express their appreciation for the actor's work. It's not yours, it's theirs. It doesn't need to be clever. It doesn't need to be its own theatrical event. It needs to present the actors in some approximate order of the size of their contribution to this particular evening. It needs to move quickly but not seem rushed. It needs to include all members of the cast. It needs to be blocked but not, in most cases, to feel like a military exercise. Be careful it isn't so long that continuing it becomes an onerous duty to the customers.

This is something you need to plan on paper, order and all. You don't want to forget someone when you are blocking it! Usually the call is blocked during the tech so the set, entrances, and exits will be well used. Time is precious in tech. Do it cleanly and clearly and don't take a long time doing it. The actors want the call, but by now they have other things on their mind.

THE FIRST PREVIEW

1. Yes, have a notetaker so you won't have to look away from the stage.

2. Something will go wrong technically; prepare yourself so you don't writhe.

3. The actors will jump laughs. They won't tomorrow night.

4. It will probably be overpaced because of the actors' adrenaline, or you'll think it is because of yours.

5. Be sure you stay there and watch the parts you know will be truly awful.

6. You'll take a lot of early notes because you're crazed. Make sure you take notes in the last third when you're dazed.

7. Once again, remember, notes for everybody.

8. Be, at the very least, basically positive with the cast afterwards. You can do useless damage if you're angry.

9. Do not give actors notes in their dressing rooms. Do it later (positive notes) or tomorrow (negative notes).

10. The design team is nervous too. Handle them gently and with respect.

OPENING DAY

To rehearse or not to rehearse? I say go for it, but keep it under three hours. Make sure what you work on gets better. That's all the actors will put up with today. Work on small sections. Only run big hunks if there are remaining tech problems. Only do a full run-through in extremis. Be cheerful, helpful, and optimistic. What's done cannot (in the main) be undone at this point. Even if it's one of those rare productions where I really feel we don't *need* to rehearse, I schedule an hour's work. And I mean work. If you have notes to give, give them and then work for a least a half hour with them on their feet. It calms and reassures a cast that you have the confidence not to demand a run-through but that right up to the last moment you are *improving* the play. We must be good they think if he or she only needs to work these ten little sections. Actors are sensitive to ritual and symbol. Your working for an hour is one and they know it.

OPENING NIGHT

Dress up, something special is happening. Looking good is a tribute to the work everyone has done. Do not bother the actors with notes. That should have been over this afternoon. If you can't help looking grim, don't go backstage. Opening night is all about the actors' confidence. Don't screw it up. Do you need to give presents? You could but what would be really lovely would be to write personal notes on nice stationary or cards. Many actors will save these notes for years, a lifetime. If you've done your job, they've been working to please you and now is the time to say you're pleased. If you're not pleased, fake it. This is not the time for devastating personal honesty. Trust me, it's not. Afterwards, when everybody goes to the bar, go along for a beer or an orange juice. Don't be above the experience. Leave having graciously settled any conflicts. You'll see each other again.

CRITICS

To read or not to read, that is the question.

1. Taking criticism is hard.

2. If you're going to read them, wait three days. You'll read them better.

3. Will you need to provide balm for injured actors? Think ahead.

4. Being murdered on Broadway made me a more text- and relationship-oriented director than the previous clever and theatrical one.

5. You'll seldom get the review you want.

6. Can critics affect your career? Yes, but probably not ultimately.

7. Never engage a critic in argument until your career is secure.

8. The reviewer reflects the views of some portion of the audience. Do you care if you appeal to that audience?

9. A bad review initiates a grieving process. Know yours so you can manage it.

10. What did you want to accomplish? Did the critic identify it? Do you assume it to be your problem or his?

In a sense the issue is too emotional and personal to respond to others' experience.

PICTURE CALL

Yes, theater is evanescent, all the more reason to ensure that good still photographs of your production exist. The director, or anyone who has the sensibility to understand the production visually, conducts the photo calls. Someone who has seen the production once often compiles in a few minutes the lists of photos to be taken. The stage manager and actors who are longing to escape for a beer are the ones who hurriedly set up the photos on the list. If you want the production recorded in accordance with your vision, it's you who compiles the list, and you, present at the photo call, who sets up each picture. Few directors do. As an aesthetic record, and possibly of historical value, these pictures might do you other favors down the road in your portfolio. Oh, a photographer will also be at work sometime during your tech. Cooperate in winning full compliance from nervous actors. These photos taken during actual performance are often the best you'll get. It's worth your while to make the extra effort on picture call.

GETTING A CAREER

1. Direct a lot, and any work you get before you have directed a lot is an unlooked-for gift.

2. Watch working directors work. Assist when possible.

3. Befriend playwrights. Help them get readings and workshops. Become their director of choice.

4. In smaller theaters, trade skills for opportunities. "I'll dramaturg your next two productions if I can direct in your Midnight Series."

5. When you're on a road trip, make appointments to chat with the artistic directors. Ask how entry-level directors can start at their theater.

6. When you have good work showing, beat down doors to get people who can help you to see it. Be a bother if necessary.

7. Compile a mailing list of people at theaters where you want to work. Let them know what you're doing four times a year.

8. Suggest projects to theaters interested in you, and keep suggesting.

9. Make your own projects.

10. Real talent will out.

The Director's Homework

THE DIRECTOR'S HOMEWORK

Everyone in theater dreads (and gossips about) the unprepared director. But, how to prepare? What's to be done before the designer's meetings, auditions, and the first rehearsal? Well you're going to want to deduce what the author intended the play to be about, and, no less important, what *you* think it's about. This is primary because the entire production process is the delivery system for the meaning. What's the story of the play? What's the meaning of the story? How can I theatricalize both? What do the characters want? How do the characters relate? How do those things deliver the meaning? Where in the text do the key points and moments lie? How do those moments relate to the theme? This work done, we can proceed to the practical details of design and later, the process of the actors. Too much obsession with detail before the big questions have been asked and answered is likely to produce thin and obvious work. Brace yourself, this preparation takes a goodly number of hours, but oh the agony if you skip this step. When I was young and clueless, I once read and conceived a Shakespeare on a five-hour flight and went into rehearsal the next morning. The results were thin and obvious!

MORE HOMEWORK

Let's be even more specific:

1. Read the play several times without conceptualizing. Imbibe it.

2. Do a list of key circumstances (see vocabulary) and ask yourself about their impact on the major characters.

3. Do a short biography of each character based in the circumstances of the text. What's there in the lines and situations, not what you imagine.

4. How do the characters change during the course of the play?

5. Describe the key relationships to a friend as if they were people you knew and were gossiping about.

6. What does each major character want above all?

7. Try writing your current idea of the play's theme in a single sentence.

8. In what specific ways will your production be theatrical?

9. What are the mistakes you want to avoid?

10. Now read the play and visualize it.

UNDERSTANDING YOUR AUDIENCE

An example: Actors Theatre of Louisville where I was artistic director for thirty years produced (surprise) an annual *Christmas Carol*. After fifteen years of watching various versions, I decided to direct my own vision of the story, which centered around the sociological evils of the Industrial Revolution. I did it on a bare stage as the Christmas fantasy of the poor. Not only was this version roundly hated by adults ("We want our *Christmas Carol* back"), it was completely baffling and boring to the 50 percent of the audience who were (how had I forgotten?) under twelve years old!

Now the question we need to mull together is what responsibility I had in that situation to my own creativity and to the audience's needs and expectations. Any theater you work in will have audiences with expectations, ones particular to those circumstances with ramifications for the play you're directing. Do you ignore them? Do you address them? What play are you doing now, and where, and for whom?

READING FROM THE CHARACTER'S VIEWPOINT

After analyzing the text, finding meanings that affect and stimulate me and thinking about theme I find it relaxing and enjoyable to read from the character's viewpoint. In a large-cast play I single out five or six major roles. In a small cast I'll do them all. I don't even pretend to take the larger view. I try to read from the character's perspective of situations and events. How does Olga in *Three Sisters* view Vershin's arrival? What does she think about her brother André's relationship to Natasha? How does she react to Irina's plan to marry and go off with Tusenbach.

I can always count on the fact that when I've finished these character reads I feel far more confident about my grasp on the play. If I find myself at sea with a particular character (now, I really do this!) I write every one of their lines on paper in order but with no one else's dialogue included. Reading through what they say from beginning to end usually clarifies my understanding of them. Of all the text work I might suggest, this is flat-out the most fun.

READING FOR THE CHARACTER'S HEART

You've read the play until the story's twists and turns are familiar. You feel you have a grasp of the dynamics of the key relationships. Now read the play once through for each substantial character, listening to their hearts. What are their hopes, their dreams, their fears? What do they long for? What need has been thwarted when they're angry? What loss do they mourn when they're sad? Where do they get their emotional sustenance? Directors who do not involve themselves with the feelings of the characters produce work that seems brittle, emotionally illogical, and alienated. Imagine someone you know well in a difficult and emotional situation. Probably you can easily project what they might do and how it would affect them. Now put one of the characters in the same situation and imagine the result. It isn't only the actors who need to be inside the characters' skins. Read for the heart.

THE MOMENT CHAIN

As we are no doubt agreed that some moments are more important than others, the question becomes, which ones? One way to discover the answer is to do a moment chain. Try to find two dozen moments in the text (this includes lines said) that if they were played in order would basically tell both the narrative and emotional story of the play. At the very least you're going to want to give those moments particular focus and importance. You can do the same thing for each important role using six to twelve moments.

Does this solve our original question? In part, and it gives us a sense of the acted structure of the work from which we can begin, until we discover further. The director is eternally on the hunt for the moments that illuminate or contain the seeds from which the play grows. We want the key moments of story and character to detonate and resonate.

CONCEPT

We use this word a lot. What does it mean? Concept is a theatrical means of presenting the play to the audience. It can mean a production done in rehearsal clothes. It can mean the characters in *Midsummer Night's Dream* become circus performers. It can mean speaking the subtext, or moving the play fifty years back or forward, or women playing men's roles, or on-site performance, or using elements of dance drama. The point is that concept is a way of revealing the *heart* of the play so that it lodges in the memory. *Concept* is not simply the director showing off, though his concept may be surprising or unusual. It may strip away or embellish, but it is a delivery system for ideas in the text and it must assist in telling the story. Does it need justification? I'm afraid it does. Can't it come to you in a dream? Absolutely, but it better be a dream of the text. Should you speak of it at the first rehearsal? Yes. And I hope with conviction.

THE NIGHTMARE
PRODUCTION

It helps to articulate the mistakes you *don't* want this production to have, to clarify what you *don't* want to do. Can you visualize these mistakes? What would be the misbegotten idea behind them? What sort of acting would ruin it? What emphasis would make it, in your eyes, vulgar? What would be the most obvious mistake about the central idea? How might you misconceive the major character? What style would render the play monstrous? Is there a kind of physicality that would damage your production? Defining what it is *not* often gets you more than halfway to what it *is*. Obviously this assists in avoiding the mistakes you've catalogued. This is a process you might engage in once you have examined the play well through several readings. You can sometimes spend a hilarious and instructive hour by running an imagined film of your nightmare version as you read through it. At the very least it allows you to make a different set of mistakes than those you can imagine.

RESEARCH

I prefer doing and setting plays in the age of photography. Why? For the architectural or emotional design of the sets you can draw on thousands of details and possibilities by looking at one hundred photographs from the place and period. As to costumes, you get to see how real people wore and adapted clothes to their needs. In photography, You get a real sense of character from life itself. Yes, it's a tuxedo like any other 1970s tuxedo, but he's wearing it with cowboy boots! The same with props. Photographs of the interior of Ozark gas stations reveal the objects that will give an authentic sense of place to a play. Photographs bear out that life *is* stranger than fiction. Ask for this research from your designers (not catalogues please!), and see if your sense of the characters and place isn't transformed.

YOUR LIFE

Your life goes with you into rehearsal and is revealed everywhere in your work. It is a truism but we must find our life in the plays we do, for otherwise they become exercises in technique. When you're having a difficult time with character, or situation, or the emotion generated you need to rifle through your experiences for a parallel. I daresay you can only understand the play in this way. Even better, these parallels engage you, and you will always do better work out of a profound and personal interest (in this case, literally, your self-interest). Rummaging through your experiences and pairing them with the text gives you a powerful tool for interesting the actors in the scene and stimulating their own personalization. My work on *Antony and Cleopatra* was hopeless until I compared my own experience of authority with that in the play (I was running a theater not a kingdom or empire) and understood how precious a real intimacy then became. Such quiet time with the text and your life needn't be revealed to anyone; it's your understanding that will be.

STYLE

Style, for the director, is some unifying physicality, rhythm, set of manners, relationship to the audience, or means of theatricality that defines the presentation of the text. It may be a set of behaviors defined by the dress and manners of a period. It may be an invented vocabulary or set of gestures. It may be doing the play while admitting it is a play. It may be a formal way the actors relate to each other or the audience. It may be a stage translation of painterly technique or the imitation of admired masters. The important thing here is to unify. Once you have established a set of physical, visual, or aural rules for your production, don't break them to solve a little problem in Act III. No matter how anarchic your take, it has boundaries. Respect them. A style may be based on research or flat-out invented by the director. It is apt when it reveals the text's meanings and inopportune when (no matter how theatrical) it does not. Style is a delivery system for meaning, not a substitute for it. You must ask if this production will have a style, and, if so, how will it be defined. Style has boundaries. No boundaries, no style.

THE GROUND PLAN CHECKLIST

A ground plan: where the doors, windows, furniture, set pieces, and so forth, are placed.

1. Check flow. Is there a reason to go everywhere?

2. Is there more than one way to get to things? It helps.

3. Is there a way to use the bottom ten percent of the stage? Is there something to do when you get there?

4. Can you vary where people are placed to have conversations?

5. What things imagined on the fourth wall will help the blocking?

6. Is the playing space cluttered or austere, and which is better for the play?

7. Does the ground plan need to be symbol or metaphor?

8. Do you need more levels for sight-lines or composition?

9. Does it make architectural sense? Do you care?

10. Are there sight-line problems?

11. Are you going to need to get someone down on the floor? Will they be seen?

12. If acting is doing, build the doing into the ground plan.

13. Do the doors properly spread the blocking?

14. Will the ground plan encourage both straight crosses and arcs?

15. Read the play. Imagine. Revise.

ANYTHING IS WHAT
YOU SAY IT IS

The directorial power to establish meaning is awesome. If you say when a woman touches her elbow to her knee it means she is hungry, that's what it will mean to us in your production. If you say that a bowl of pebbles collected at great risk is the food, so be it. If you say a hooded figure can kill by blowing a kiss to anyone on stage, so be it. If you say that when it's dark it's light and when it's light it's dark, that everyone walks in the air, and that all the characters in the play are gorillas in eighteenth-century dress, that's what we think too. As a director, you are ordering the play's universe as you wish to make the play's point. If you are rigorous, we will accept that order for the two hours' traffic. The point in the end will be what beauty and meaning you deliver and whether it rewards us both emotionally and intellectually. As you sit at home planning the production, imagine varying the rules of the known universe to create your telling and emotional points. What will the play be when you have invented its vocabulary?

PREBLOCKING

Should you or shouldn't you? I started my career with large casts, *The Crucible, Volpone, The Rivals,* and was definitely in over my head. At night I would sit in my room with a ground plan and pennies that I covered with tape with the characters' initials penned onto them. Then I wrote the pennies' blocking into the margins of my script. The actors' initiative became a problem, of course. When someone wanted to move right instead of left, several pages of my night's work would be destroyed. My suggestion to the young director is that any scene with four people or less can be blocked onstage with the actors' help. Intermediate scenes with four to eight probably need repetitive visualization before you do them. The large group scenes may send you back to the pennies until further experience trains your eye. All blocking assumes the director's mastery of character and situation.

PROPS

After I've read the play I'm going to do five or six times, I always make a list I call "things." These are the objects already called for in the text as well as those I've thought of that may be present in the spaces the playwright has described and those that may clarify a moment or idea, signify beyond themselves, give the actor something interesting to do, or get the laugh. It's one of my favorite lists and one that always gets my imagination pumping. I try to have some of them around early in the blocking process as a stimulus, both for me and the actor.

Later on in your production an actor may seem lost or marginalized and the problem may be that they have nothing to *do*. Sometimes I huddle with the actor, "Jack, what else could he be doing in the kitchen?" Sometimes I walk up and put an object in the actor's hand. Sometimes the problems are narrative. We want to see her to carve the chicken with the knife that she uses to kill her brother in the final moments. And, of course, they can define character. Make the list.

THE DISCONNECT

There are times when logic is a theatrical bore, and cause and effect a commonplace. Many great directors disconnect logic to create a different kind of perception for the audience. Whether you have a talent for these techniques only experiment can reveal. It is important for us to know that there are other theatrical worlds. What if gesture and text didn't support each other but were two different tracks? What if we disrupt the physical logic of an ordinary room? What if we change the meanings of the gestural vocabulary? What if we disconnect psychology and speech? What if we load the speech, the space, the physical symbolically? What if we insert elements of the random in our careful structures? There is fascinating theater to be made outside our current logic. Follow such experiments in our profession, see the work, and, if it attracts you, experiment in secure situations. Remember, however, that few talents make careers outside the traditional boundaries. If your talent lies there, good, but don't remain an acolyte in a system you only mimic.

NEW USES FOR THE FAMILIAR

Realism has expanded. Have you?

1. One space is often many spaces.

2. One object is often many objects.

3. Time is often expanded to use many periods simultaneously.

4. The role may not be sex-specific.

5. What would happen if everything was much slower? Much faster?

6. What if we disorder or reorder common psychology?

7. Mix cultural behaviors.

8. Invent gestural vocabularies.

9. Remove emphasis.

10. Find new uses for simple objects.

11. Revel in repetition.

12. Excise sentiment.

13. Play with, alter chronology.

14. Assign different values to acts and results.

Question your theatrical assumptions.

THE NONREALISTIC OR SELECTIVE GROUND PLAN

We don't need complete rooms or complete football fields. One easy chair with lamp and door can make the living room and one bench and a bucket the field. One chandelier can create Versailles. Leaving realism allows metaphor to flourish. What three things can create your prison, your Manhattan, your space shuttle? What single object means high school? Another way to look at things is to use real objects but distort their organization. How about a table with two chairs on top of it. A refrigerator with a phone booth inside it. If we do these things, what meaning do we make with this reorganization of reality? Yes, put the bed upright on the wall, suspend the sofa in midair, but draw meaning from it. Austerity is often the mark of the mature talent, but why not become acquainted with it in your youth? I remember a fascinating production of *Measure for Measure* with no set and one chair. The use of the chair became an icon for justice, its overturning the destruction of same. Sometimes the ground plan can say everything you want to say about the play.

TO DECONSTRUCT

When this word appeared as a vital part of our theatrical language, it sowed confusion. What was a deconstructed classic? How did the director go about it? What was the idea at work? Deconstruction exposes the structural ideas and the concepts and assumptions inherent in them: you see the play in a different light and its inner workings exposed. Because any literary structure has in it assumptions, those assumptions may be seen from a current perspective to contain different meanings. The romantic comedy of the 1950s may now reveal racism and sexism unnoticed at the time. The deconstruction holds these elements to the light and comments on them. The play may have meant one thing at Elizabeth's court and another in a Chicago production in 2001. An example is *Taming of the Shrew* transformed from an amusing battle of the sexes to a cautionary tale of physical abuse.

SCENE GROUPS

As a director our rehearsal schedule usually looks like this:

10–11	Act I Scene 7
11–12	Act 2 Scene 4
12–1	Act 2 Scene 9

Now there comes a time after you have blocked and worked each of the scenes when that becomes the wrong kind of schedule. When you work scenes in isolation, you often make choices that seem good for the scene but then turn out to be too much of something when placed in the context of the play. The answer to this problem isn't simply more run-throughs. Instead, set the necessary hours to work through twenty continuous pages, stopping and fixing whenever necessary but doing so with regard to the whole. The most obvious version of this problem is that a rapid pace may seem useful and interesting when working a single scene but will seem forced and flat when set into other scenes where you've made the same kind of choices. In the final third of rehearsal, work in context whenever possible.

AFTERWORD

I love the theater's traditions, the sense that we could have sat in Molière's and Shakespeare's rehearsals and made sense of the craft in process. These pages contain some of that eternal craft and a good many of my personal prejudices. Some will fall in with yours, and others . . . well, the good thing about tips is that you can always ignore them. I hope you will remember that the play is central, the text provides the rules of the game, and that delivering the play is a group activity in which the director is first among equals but only that. In all my travels I have seen the work of perhaps six directorial minds that have found a "new way," but I have seen a thousand who would have benefited from received knowledge. Thinking about directing as a craft demystifies a process that may be complex but can be parsed, understood, and practiced. Sometimes I am of the opinion that we are attracted to the idea that it should be incapable of definition. It's not. The craft can be learned, and that's a lot.